To
Carol
much love
and admiration
xo   Jack

MW01598960

CATHOLIC CHURCH? WHY NOT?

VOLUME 1

PAUL D'AMOUR

authorHOUSE®

AuthorHouse™
1663 Liberty Drive
Bloomington, IN 47403
www.authorhouse.com
Phone: 833-262-8899

Published by AuthorHouse 04/19/2021

ISBN: 978-1-6655-1336-4 (sc)
ISBN: 978-1-6655-1335-7 (e)

Library of Congress Control Number: 2021900609

Print information available on the last page.

This book is printed on acid-free paper.

CONTENTS

"Some men see things as they are,
And say why, I dream of things
That never were, and say why not."

Robert F. Kennedy

INTRODUCTION

I began writing these journals when I was recently assigned as pastor of a parish church called St. Francis of Assisi. It is situated in a small prairie rural bedroom community (population 1,870) identified by three working elevators a major railway line and a large regional weekend farmers market. The town is located 45 minutes by car from a large city (pop. 115,000) that I grew up in, and where my parents, siblings and their families live. I am quite anxious about my adjustment from working and living in an urban parish with Father Mike, to a rural parish lifestyle where I live and work alone. Six weeks ago, I was asked by Bishop Ben, my boss (officially he is called Bishop Benedict) to assume the pastoral duties of St. Francis of Assisi Catholic parish. Two weeks ago, I arrived, and since then I have done nothing that I am accustomed to doing other than celebrating masses on Saturday and Sunday at St. Francis, and at St. Joseph, a small neighboring rural church. In addition, I have been slowly getting a sense of the community, namely by introducing myself to the doctors and nurses at the local hospital, the police officers at the RMCP office, the owner of the grocery store, the principal at the local high school (it has a fitness facility utilized by the community), the editor of the local newspaper, the owner of the hardware, and checking out the quality of the local restaurants. A lot of activity in a short period of time. As this is July with the summer break from school and regular routines, many parishioners are away on holidays or at summer cottages. Life is slower than usual, permitting my introduction to the community in a leisurely way. But still, I am anxious.

I am writing these journal entries in a confidential manner because I want to protect my Bishop, my priestly colleagues, my parishioners, my family and my friends from being unduly exposed, criticized, or put at risk in one way or another for my views on church. Priests are neither public figures nor encouraged to be so. The priesthood is a closed-personnel organization, like police and military organizations. The Bishops and church leaders use command and control to manage the day to day church activities. This lack of transparency and resulting lack of accountability is fraught with dangers for the church, as has occurred during the recent sexual abuses crises. I hope to publish these journals at some point. Why? Most people, I believe, (including myself before I became a priest), do not know how priests live their daily lives: what they do? how they work? what they do for fun and enjoyment. In addition, the sexual abuse scandals and their cover-up by church leaders, their abysmal treatment of women and the LGBTQ community, in my opinion, has resulted in many priests going underground and becoming invisible. I think it has also contributed to a mass exodus from the church particularly of younger people. I hope to begin changing that image by my attitudes and practice. I hope my social work education and emphasis on being non-judgmental will be an asset.

I also have a confession to make. Part of my need for confidentiality is that I am not your typical Catholic priest. While I am supposed to be a model Catholic, there are many teachings of the Church that I struggle with and do not teach. I am a firm believer in the fundamentals of the Gospels to love and serve God and our neighbor, the practice of tolerance, of forgiveness, and all that they entail. But this message has been over shadowed over the years by exclusivity, a blind acceptance of "obey and pay" as dictated by our patriarchal, celibate church leadership. A patriarchal male priesthood dominates the Church today whereas more of our membership is comprised of females who have little or no voice. In my opinion, we spend too much time and effort teaching the rules of the church particularly about birth control and other sexual practices that seem horribly out of date with the daily challenges of family life, holding down a job and enjoying the few fleeting pleasures that come along in life. That is my secret. I suspect there are many priests like me, but they have been thoroughly intimidated over the years from speaking up.

CHAPTER 1

My Bishop Ben and Max
(Tuesday, June 12, a month earlier)

My Bishop is very atypical and very down to earth. He is not aloof or other-worldly. His name is Benedict but is known as just simply Bishop Ben. He lives in a 2-bedroom apartment within a short walk to the Cathedral where he celebrates an early morning mass. He has an office near the Cathedral and his apartment. He cooks his own meals (Italian)except for lunches, which he takes at the Cathedral. He has a dog named Max, (a rescue dog), a 5-year-old black Labrador (that carries a salivary old tennis ball that is always in its mouth everywhere it goes), and his constant companion even when he is celebrating mass. Bishop Ben looks quite fit, has a military haircut, over six feet tall, with a very pleasant face and is known to walk everywhere he can for exercise. He is supposedly younger than I am by a few years. He is very laid back, calm, and an excellent listener. He has been casually dressed when I have met him in his office; sometimes in a suit and roman collar, sometimes in colorful shirt and black slacks. I am told that he is a big football fan and will wear to work his favorite team's jersey on a game day. He certainly is breaking the mold. As I remember, his advice to me was:

1. The first thing in the morning, once you get your wits about you, pray, dedicate yourself to doing everything, even the smallest act, out of love for the Lord and your neighbor, and perform them as best you can;

2. Make a daily task list either the night before or in the morning and check off the items that you accomplished at the end of your day;
3. Try to do something every day that is beneficial to someone;
4. Your evening prayer is vitally important. It is an opportunity to review your day, do a thorough examination of conscience and count God the Father's many blessings that you experience that day;
5. Reach out to everyone in the community from doctors, policemen, school teachers, mail person and the pizza parlor;
6. Learn to relax into the silence and the slowness of small-town living, and listen to the Holy Spirit who will begin to whisper wisdom into your ear;
7. Get to know the physical layout of the community by walking it. Get some exercise every day. Do pushups. You may want to get yourself an indoor exercise bike;
8. Organize meetings with the men of the parish, the Catholic Women's League and parish council. Listen to them. They will help you adjust and will tell you their needs;
9. Avoid too much TV time;
10. Do not celebrate Mass alone;
11. Avoid drinking alcohol alone;
12. Do not drink alcohol when carrying out parish visits despite the pressure;
13. Avoid providing counselling of any kind. Leave that to the professionals. Do not have any contact with a woman or child, alone in your rectory. Do so only in a public place, a library or coffee shop
14. No hugging of children or young adults. Be careful about hugging or touching unless it is your parents or siblings;

15. Cook large quantities of food that you can eat as leftovers and freeze for other occasions when you do not have time to cook;
16. I would like to see you every month for a review of your parish work; and
17. He scheduled my next meeting for early August.

Father in heaven, help me to be a good priest and not screw up this new assignment. Take care of Bishop Ben, my family and my parishioners. Thank you for everything you do for me; my good life and the many opportunities you give to me.

CHAPTER 2

Notes for a future parish bulletin #1 Wednesday, July 13

My fellow parishioners, my name is Father Cam Wilson. Please call me Cam. I am honored to be asked by Bishop Ben to be your parish priest. It is a privilege to serve you. I know that you have not had a resident priest for some time. I hope in time to win your trust and support. This is a wonderful opportunity for me and I feel very blessed. I am forty-eight years of age and a "newbie" priest. While I hope not to make too many glaring mistakes, I hope you will find it in your hearts to be both understanding and forgiving when I do. I have much to learn and request your candid advice whenever you see me "crossing over the line."

You probably do not know that I was married for many years until my wife sadly passed away from ALS in her mid 30's. I have degrees in social work as well as theology. Before becoming a priest, I worked for some years in the development of low-income housing and emergency women's shelters.

I hope that over time, you will inform me of your expectations, your needs and the things about our church that disappoint you. I do not promise to address all your concerns but I will try my hardest to do so.

What bothers me terribly and might bother you as well, is that many persons are currently abandoning the church and their Catholic practice. Many young people, upon leaving home, never go to church except to fulfill social obligations at Christmas, Easter, weddings and funerals. I will be asking your advice on how to change this situation.

I want to conclude my words by telling you how much I admire each and every one of you. It is not easy being a practicing Catholic in today's world. A religious or spiritual practice is not in vogue any more. It requires a conscious effort, a deep faith and discipline, to develop a rational and meaningful practice of our faith. We are out of step with what society in general measures success for its members, such as a big job, a big house, a big car, a summer house, all parts of a very rich and materialistic lifestyle. I heard a philosopher say, that we spend the first forty years of our lives acquiring as many material possessions as possible and the last forty years trying to let go of them. Let's work together to rediscover the joys and the happiness of a Catholic way of life.

CHAPTER 3

Visiting my family (Sunday, July 15)

After the last mass on Sunday, I regularly drive to the city and spend the rest of the day with my family and have Monday off. I do not have to concern myself with the Sunday collections that most priests I know deal with as the parish council manages it. My family, comprised of my parents, two siblings, their partners and their four children are very important to me. Mondays is usually a day off for parish priests. Weekends are busy times in a parish; the parish community congregates on weekends, people get married on weekends, and other parish milestones occur on Sundays. Monday is a recovery day. Sunday night family dinners for my family have been a tradition for as long as I can remember. One had to have a very important reason to miss them if you were in the city. My parents, both in their seventies, still enjoy hosting these meals for the family. My dad and my older brother are in the hardware and building supply business together. My brother's wife is a kindergarten teacher. My little sister, is a high school English teacher, and her husband works in a bank. She is very significant in my life. She was the best person with whom I could talk about my grief after my wife Wendy died, and later about my relationships with women when I was feeling vulnerable. Now I can talk to her when I am feeling lonely, tired, vulnerable and fearful to the kind and innocent attention from female friends and parishioners. I really depend on her and she has always accommodated me whenever I am feeling insecure. I have heard many dreadful stories of priests using alcohol and sex to alleviate their loneliness and fears. After dinner, we sit around, play cards and share our daily activities. I still enjoy a sleepover at my parents. After a slow breakfast on Monday, I usually try to get some exercise for an hour, have lunch with some priest colleagues, visit a hospital if a parishioner is there, go to confession (priests are encouraged to go to confession regularly and have a priest-counselor with whom one can discuss personal spiritual matters and get wise advice), have dinner with my parents and return to the parish. I return with frozen food my mother has prepared for me, including hearty soups, casseroles and frozen home-made burgers.

My goals for the week are:

1. Find a university course either in the city or on line either in history or the Bible.
2. Reach out to the ministers of the local churches. I think it would be good for me to meet with them once a month to pray, be supportive of one another and study.
3. Have coffee with the RCMP officers to find out about the town culture from their perspective.
4. Organize my office and establish a daily routine for prayer (and meditation), study and exercise.
5. Organize meetings for September of the Pastoral Council, the Catholic Women's league and the Men's Group.

Thank you, Father, in heaven for my mother and her generous food parcels. Thank you for my family who know me only too well and do not let me take myself too seriously. Please keep them in good health. Thank you for your continuing care of me and giving me this wonderful parish to work in.

CHAPTER 4

Joe and Mary (Thursday, July 19)

During my first year as a pastoral assistant in St. Michael's Parish, I met Joe and Mary, (not their real names) an older couple who usually attended daily mass. After months of greeting them as they left the church, I approached them and asked if I could have coffee with them. They readily agreed and I was invited to come to their home the following day at 10:00 am. I told them my story of my career, my marriage, my wife's untimely death and my new role of a priest. I admitted that I was troubled by the current image of the church and its message that seemed so out of touch and irrelevant to so many people both inside and outside the church.

When I finally finished my introduction, they smiled with a certain knowingness and replied that they would like to share their story as well. Joe was a semi-retired businessman, the owner of a chain of mobile home parks. His retirement was precipitated by heart disease. He was married to his first wife who died of cancer, leaving him to raise 4 children on his own. After his children had left home, he fortuitously met Mary in a bookstore. She was a school principal. Today they are both happily married and retired. After an hour, I felt that I had overstayed my welcome. As I got up to leave. I asked how if I could come by again next week for another visit and chat about church. They quickly agreed and that was the beginning of a series of regular visits, where we talked about the inner spiritual strength and beauty of Catholicism and where they shared their opinions on how the church could become more attractive and relevant. I have made the following brief notes of their key suggestions:

1. Simplify the message and the rules. The message, in their opinion, should be love, tolerance and mercy. The key practice should be service of the community. Imagine what the church would be like if we just practiced these values;
2. The church should stick with what it has historically done so well; it has a proven record of service in schools, hospitals and social services;
3. Treat parishioners as spiritual adults, not as children. Give them the benefit of the doubt if you are not sure;
4. Drop all discussion about sex in the church. There are many church leaders, even in the Vatican, who believe that these teachings are two hundred years out of date. The church has lost much of its moral authority because of sexual abuse scandals and its teachings on sexuality. Encourage your parishioners to seek sexual advice from their family doctor;
5. Rely on the pastoral council to help you run the parish;
6. Short homilies, ten minutes max;
7. If the church needs rules, use the ten commandments. Skip the rest, and
8. The priest should be a welcoming presence in the parish, expressing the Church's core message of love, tolerance and forgiveness.

Father in heaven, thank you for Joe and Mary, please keep them healthy and close to your heart. Thank you, Father, for your many blessings: my good health, my supportive family, my Bishop, Father Mike, my colleagues and my parishioners.

CHAPTER 5

Update on my personal tasks (Tuesday, July 24)

a) I discovered that the Anglican Church of Canada offers courses in scripture by correspondence. I have signed up for a Fall course on the Old Testament. I have received the permission from Bishop Ben who cautioned me that while I will be learning the protestant interpretation of these texts, I should do my assignments from a Catholic perspective. He referred me a friend of his, a Bishop in Ontario who has a PhD in scripture studies from Rome and Jerusalem. If I am having questions that are not being answered to my satisfaction by the teaching staff, he has already cleared it with his friend that I can call him. I am excited.

b) Lunch with the RCMP officers.

   I invited them for a Gregorio's pizza lunch at the rectory. Two officers showed up, Sergeant Ron Walker (no relation) (but it certainly can't hurt me to be known as a Walker when dealing with problems in this commuity) and Officer Melanie Campbell. Walker has been stationed here for three years while Campbell just one year. To my inquiry into what keeps them busy, they replied that they have the usual small-town issues like an occasional domestic violence episode, alcohol and drug issues with young people, young people both men and women car racing on back roads, some rural crime and family problems related to poverty. They manage drunkenness by incarceration for a day, car racing by huge fines, domestic violence particularly where the male is causing the problem by incarcerating him for two days. A unique police practice of managing crime in a small town. No courts are needed for these small problems. The community also likes this policing style. Where serious cases involve going to trial, they transport these individuals to the city. In their opinion, the community is easy to work in because the farmers are reasonably well off as compared to some other detachments where they have worked. I inquired what they thought that the parish could do for the community. After some thought, he said that programs for youth, ages 14 to 25 that required discipline and structure would benefit their work and the community.

c) Coffee with the resident Anglican priest.

I had coffee at the local Tim Horton's with the Rev. Mrs. Claire Meadows, an Anglican priest, a very pleasant, down to earth, red-headed woman. She has been in this parish for 10 years. Her husband is a science teacher at the high school. They have two adult children at university. She said that they love the community. It is safe and that they rarely to need lock their doors. The community is very cooperative and comes together easily when there is a need. She said however, that her parish is struggling both financially and in maintaining its membership. Christianity is not seen as attractive or even beneficial any more. The small community of twenty parishioners is not able to sustain a large church and a priest. She said her parish, St. Gabriel's, struggles to keep the lights on, let alone pay her salary. She feels that the church will probably be sold and the small group of parishioners will meet in homes or in a local school. She expects that her Bishop will end up selling their church as there is quite a demand for churches by the growing number of immigrant religious groups. I responded by asking how she would feel sharing a Catholic church for weekend services and other events. She replied that she would love it but would need to run it past her parish board.

When I asked her about organizing a prayer group of the various church ministers, she thought it was a great idea and said she would be glad to help. She knew the United Church minister, a Mrs. Joan White. There were only the three churches in town but perhaps they could be joined by members of their respective congregations. I agreed. We ended by targeting late September for our first meeting to be held in her home. I would host the October meeting.

F ather in heaven, thank you for your continuing daily care of me, the finding of an online course in Sacred Scripture and the Bishop's support of the course from the Anglican Church. Thank you for the meeting with the two RCMP officers: Walker and Campbell. Keep them safe. Protect them as they daily put themselves in harm's way for us. Thank you for arranging the meeting with Claire. I feel very excited about my future relationships with my Protestant colleagues.

CHAPTER 6

Meeting with Fred Bartlett, the chairman of the Parish Council, (Thursday, July 26)

F red appeared at my door fifteen minutes after I phoned him. A big man well over six feet, wearing overalls and could have been a lineman on a professional football team. In spite of that, he seemed more of a cuddly bear in spite of his vise-like hand shake. He is slow-talking and is married to Thelma who is a member of the Catholic Women's League (a Catholic women's organization) in the parish. He began by saying that now St. Francis has a resident parish priest, the parish had finally arrived. He grew up in the area and farms over twelve hundred acres, all in grain or food crops. He admitted that he is fifty-one years of age and his two sons Chad and Chuck, aged twenty and twenty-one, help him run the farm. They are not married and worry him as they are known to party a lot and not come home weekend nights. On the whole, they are hard-working and responsible when on the farm. He says that they drive to the city where they attend mass. He does not check up on them and nor should he. He feels that they need to grow up by making a few mistakes. He is very likeable and approachable.

I gave him a quick overview of my background and quickly turned the conversation back to the parish. He made no comments on my background. Should I be concerned by his lack of response? Would he welcome me or distance himself from this unusual individual? Five-years ago, he continued, they put an addition on the church to accommodate a growing Catholic population. They did it as an incentive for the Bishop to give them a resident priest. It worked didn't it, he said with a smile. The Bishop approved the bank loan and they still have $60,000.00 left to pay of the original $200,000.00 loan. The other matter of debate on the parish council is the need for a small Blessed Sacrament chapel walled off within the church that would be suitable for small weekday masses. This would reduce their heating bills and help pay off their loan sooner. The Bishop has not discouraged the idea. He asked if I have heard of a mobile home being used as a rectory and how I like living in it? I replied that even though I had never lived in one before, I really liked it. The mobile home was very spacious and comfortable. I inquired about the number of parishioners. He was not sure but would make it a point to find out. I inquired how many women were on the parish council? He replied none. I then asked him how he and the parish council would feel to have an equal representation of men and women on the council? He acknowledged that it was a good idea. I will put a notice in the next parish bulletin inviting women in the parish to join. He responded positively that October would be a good starting date. We could use the September meeting to introduce the current council of the proposed change.

He continued that the parish council was thinking of putting me or the next priest on a monthly salary that would include accommodation, food, car allowance, telephone, internet and money for education/pension. He asked me what I thought of this idea? I said that it seemed fine with me, but had he talked about this with the Bishop? No, not yet. I encouraged him to do so soon. I then told him about my lunch with the RCMP and their suggestions for youth programs. I explained that I had coffee at Tim Horton's with the Anglican priest, Mrs. Claire Meadows. After explaining their precarious financial situation, I asked Fred how he and the parish council would feel about sharing St Francis with the Anglicans. He looked at me carefully for a long minute and said that in his opinion there could be some major benefits but they would need to pay their share of the cleaning, heat and other expenses. I agreed and requested that we put it on the September agenda of the parish council.

I asked him where I could buy a stationary exercise bike. He suggested that I go to a fitness store in the city and purchase one there.

Father in heaven, thank for Fred, such a gentleman, businessman and farmer. Bless him, his wife and two sons. Bless the Pastoral Council and guide them in their deliberations and decisions. Thank you for your continuing care of me; help me not to screw up my first assignment. Please continue to care for my family and my parishioners.

CHAPTER 7

A meeting with the Chair of the Catholic Women's League (CWL), (Friday, July 27)

We had agreed by phone to meet at Tim Horton's, my new favorite safe meeting place. Mabel stood up as I entered and introduced herself as Mrs. Mabel Armstrong, housewife, mother, grandmother, retired nurse and chair of the Catholic Women's League in the parish. She is tall, well dressed with every hair in place and quite serious looking, much like I remember Sister Margaret, the principal of my elementary school. I introduced myself with my practiced, now well-honed speech. When I inquired about the things that occupied her organization, she replied emphatically that her little group ten members were dedicated to supporting the Church's teaching against pre-marital sex, divorce, abortion, same sex marriage, artificial birth control and assisted murder. She took my breath away. I have never heard someone speak with such authority and confidence on these matters. I asked if this occupied all of the CWL's time and energy? She replied that they write a lot of letters to members of Parliament, even warning them that come the next election, their seats will not be secure if they waffle on these matters. She expressed outrage at the leaders of the major political parties, some allegedly good Catholics, who have made the matter of an abortion a woman's personal choice. I said that I thought it was because they did not want to impose their religious values on others. She ignored my response and said that they hoped to have some articles published in the local newspaper in the Fall. I explained to her that one of my major pastoral concerns was the promotion of good marital relationships as they can have a positive influence on children for a lifetime. If good marital relationships are not well modelled, they can be at the root of a multiplicity of family problems, I said speaking like a good social worker. This was an opportunity to explain to her my social work education and career. I also told her that I would like the CWL members to articulate what women want in marriage or what makes a good marriage. Similarly, I will be asking the men's group the same questions. The answers to these questions could hopefully become the bases for improving marriages both in the parish and in the community. With the permission of both groups, I may want to eventually publish these ideas in the local newspaper. I asked her what she thought of this idea? She remained silent for what seemed like an eternity and said simply, let's discuss it at our September meeting. I agreed. I also mentioned to her what the RCMP told me about the need for programs for the 15 to 25 age group. She thought that need was very interesting. I then thanked her for her time. As I walked back to the rectory, I realized that I am going to have my work cut out to bump this group off their sex agenda in favor of more community-focused activities. I liked her idea of using the local newspaper to promote our Catholic agenda.

Father in heaven, please give me good judgment, the knowledge and the wisdom so that I may love you more and serve you and my parishioners better. Continue to care for Mabel and her CWL colleagues. Guide me in my dealing with them as they are so well-meaning.

CHAPTER 8

Meeting with the President of the Parish Men's Club. (Friday, July 27)

Bill McMillan the owner of the Ford dealership, is the current president. A sunny outgoing man, a typical car salesman; chatty and friendly. He confessed that the men's group only meets on an as need basis. They help the parish council carry out their tasks. He mentioned that the men's group were given the role to arrange accommodation for the new resident priest. They discovered that a mobile home was possible and could become a permanent structure beside the church. He asked how I liked living in it? While I replied that I am still getting used to it. I particularly liked the spaciousness and the new appliances. I asked him what my role should be in addition to celebrating mass and the sacraments. He hoped that my presence would give the church a friendly and an approachable face in the community. He has already heard good gossip about my interest in the broader community. While he did not have any specific ideas or suggestions, he thought that they would evolve over time. I told him that my priority was promoting good marital and family relationships. I told him about my meeting with the President of the CWL and my desire to get their members to discuss what women want from a marital partner. Furthermore, I would be sharing their comments with the men's club members. He gave me a questioning look/half smile as if to say, that is a very deep rabbit hole. I also explained that I want the men's group to enunciate what men want in a marriage too. That will be fun, he said, and I hope you do not blush easily. I told him about my meeting with the RCMP and their suggestion for youth programs. He looked interested. We discussed an agenda for the September meeting in the rectory and agreed to the following:

1. Father Cam will present himself and take questions;
2. Father Cam will ask the men's group of potential ways that the group can contribute to the vitality of the community; and,
3. What do men want in a marriage?

I also mentioned as we concluded our visit that I was going to put a small notice in the local weekly newspaper explaining who I was, my background and that I was looking forward to getting to know the community. He thought it was a good idea.

Father in heaven, here we are at the end of another day. Thank you for your care of me. Help me not to take your food, your accommodation and your priesthood for granted. Thank you for Bill today. Please care for him, his wife and family. Help them to grow in love of you and of each other.

CHAPTER 9

Core teaching #1, Love of God (Saturday/Sunday, July 28/29)

My dear friends in Christ. I want to thank you for coming to Mass today and making this Eucharistic celebration a community event. Now suppose someone in a polite conversation were to ask you what were the key Catholic teachings. What would you answer? Well, if I were asked, I would say that the message is about love and the importance of relationships. The Old and New testaments of the Bible, especially the Gospel of Matthew is very clear about this; we are to love and serve God and love and serve our neighbor. I am sure that you have heard this mandate many times if you attend mass regularly. Given that our present Pope has made the preservation and care of the environment a key focus of his papacy, I think we should add preserving and caring for the environment. St. Paul in his first letter to the Corinthian Church helps us to understand the meaning of love: "Love is kind, is not envious, or boastful or arrogant or rude. It does not insist on its own way; it is not irritable or resentful; it does not rejoice in wrongdoing but rejoices in the truth". So as followers of Christ, we can conclude that relationships, but especially family relationships, are at the core of the practice of our faith.

In St. John's Gospel and letters, he explains that God is love. It follows that where love is, God is. Doesn't that change the way you look at others, and they us. What does that tell us of the kind and loving behavior of those who do not profess Christianity?

Let's focus today on our relationship with the God. How do you perceive God? What is your image of God? For me, my image of God is the image of my uncle Bill. He lived with us for a year after my aunt died. He was very attached to her and found living alone difficult. To me, he was always kind, supportive and approachable no matter what state of mind or trouble that I was in. He never judged me. He was very reassuring and would state regularly that growing into adulthood was challenging and sometimes we make mistakes. I could talk to him about anything. So, for me, talking to God is like talking to my uncle Bill.

What do we know about God? The old testament of the Bible is filled with beautiful stories of how God has been engaged with the Jewish people beginning with Adam and Eve, Noah, Abraham, Moses. In the new testament, the four gospels show us Christ, the son of God who shares with us and understanding of his father, God the Father. Christ while he was on earth, lived and taught God the Father's patient love. You will recall the story of the lost sheep and how God is like the shepherd that will leave the ninety-nine and go in search of the sheep that is lost until he finds it. The story of the Prodigal son also illustrates how God like the prodigal son's father, lovingly welcomes us back home after we have fallen and stumbled. The Holy Spirit, the third person of the Triune God guides the church and each of us today. The Holy Spirit operates in the silence of our lives. Busy-ness and noise prevents us from hearing his wisdom.

Therefore, we believe that God created the world; the sun, the moon, the grain, the flowers, the animals and lastly us. He gave the earth to us to live in, manage and enjoy. He wants what is best for us. This teaching in no way contradicts what scientists believe about how life began, called the big bang theory. This God, this all-powerful creator of the earth, also seeks us out and wants a relationship with us. All the elements of St Paul's description of love, God manifests to each one of us. The many examples of Christ's good works are a reflection of the love of God the Father for us. In Psalm 145, God is depicted as "gracious and merciful, slow to anger and abounding in steadfast love. The Lord is good to all, and his compassion is over all that He has made".

What are the benefits of God's love in our life? We can be happier, calmer and hopeful. We can feel healed from our past mistakes. We can worry less. We can feel confident in being able to manage whatever comes along in our daily lives. We can feel an inner light and strength. We can love others better without worrying if our love will be reciprocated. We can reach out to others with confidence.

Why should we love the Lord our God? We are grateful. We acknowledge that God has given us a wonderful lifestyle. Why are we living in Canada, a land of plenty of everything? We are so privileged when compared to those living in South America, Africa and other Third world countries. We can be thankful to God for all these gifts. We can also praise God for the beauty of what we see.

How do we discover what God is doing in our lives? How do we love God in return? One way is to create some quiet time every day where we can spend one-on-one time with God in silent prayer and reflection. Just like any important personal relationship, we need to devote time to our relationship with God. We can acknowledge with thankfulness the good things that we have. We can ask God to address the needs of our families and friends. We can ask for help in our daily lives dealing with people and issues that challenge us. We can examine our conscience every day, where we can see how we failed in living up to our goal to be a better person. We ask God's forgiveness for our selfishness and failures and ask for the strength to forgive others for their failures.

Our God is sometimes described by some writers as a God of surprises. To fully appreciate the actions of God in your life, I recommend that you set aside a few moments at the end of your day to reflect on all the good things that have happened to you and to those that you love.

Father in heaven, thank you for all that you do for me. I cannot understand why I am the recipient of your abundant love and kindness. Help me to be kind and understanding of others.

CHAPTER 10

Day off (Monday, July 30)

My daily routine

6:30 am out of bed;

6:45 am morning prayer, dedicating my day to God, asking for His assistance in dealing with what arises during my day, prepare for mass and a short homily/commentary on the biblical readings;

7:30 am Mass, when scheduled in the parish;

8:00 am brief breakfast in the rectory with those who attended mass and those who have time. Then a few private minutes for a prayer of thanksgiving;

9:00 am organize my day, office work, a walk in the community or ride my stationery bike for 20-30 minutes and 20 push-ups;

11:00 am walk to the post office to pick up the mail and a newspaper;

11:45 am examination of conscience, a Jesuit practice I have picked up and find helpful;

12:00 noon, lunch of some of mother's soup and a sandwich while watching the national news;

1:00 pm more office work, study and unpacking my books and putting them into my used IKEA bookshelves;

5:00 pm organizing dinner and evening meetings;

6:00 pm dinner and TV news;

7:00 pm meetings or sports on TV. July is good baseball watching;

9:00 pm evening prayer, examination of conscience and novel reading time; and

11:00 pm lights out.

CHAPTER 11

An attempted suicide
(Friday, August 03)

At 9:00 am this Saturday morning, I had a telephone call from the hospital. A Dr. Hazelton called asking me to see a young woman who had attempted suicide. She had listed her religious affiliation as Roman Catholic. Could I please come to the hospital and visit her? I replied that I could but would need to have a female nurse attend the visit. He agreed. Upon being directed to a bright sunny office, I was introduced to Susan (not her real name) and nurse Rita. After telling her a little bit about myself, I asked her to tell me about herself. She explained that she was Australian, working in Canada on a temporary work permit. She was in her early 20's and pregnant. Her partner was a very immature young man who would not make a good husband or father. I immediately thought about Fred Bartlett's two sons, the party guys and wondered if they were involved. She was raised in foster homes in Australia and had no roots in either Canada or Australia. Given her bleak circumstances, her suicide attempt seemed more like an awkward request for help than an act of desperation. Regardless, I asked her about her plans. She replied that having an abortion would be the simplest solution. I asked her if she would consider having the baby and giving it up for adoption. She said that she would never permit her child to grow up moving from one foster home to another like what she had to endure as a child. I asked her if she would give me some time to work on a different solution to the abortion option. She reluctantly agreed. Nurse Rita advised that she would be staying at the hospital for more medical-related treatments. She assured me that the nurses would take good care of her. I thanked both of them and gave them my phone number in case they needed to call me. I reminded them that weekends are my busiest time but I would not forget my promise to find alternatives. Back at the rectory, I phoned Mabel Armstrong, President of the CWL and told her the story of this young woman. I asked if there was something that the CWL could do for her? She replied that she would like to talk to her members and get back to me. I then phoned my sister and again explained these dreadful circumstances. Sis, please suggest something, I pleaded. She asked if I was coming for dinner Sunday night. I replied yes. She said let's talk about it over dinner and assured me that there were better options to having an abortion for this lonely girl. Mabel phoned late in the afternoon to say that after consulting some of her members and given the short notice, they could not offer her a safe home where she could live out her pregnancy. The town was too small for such an option. She thought that finding an understanding home in a large city would be better at giving her both anonymity and the opportunity to learn some employment skills that would benefit her regardless what choice she made. She did offer some financial support for her during the pregnancy and for a year after the baby was born. I was ecstatic. I could hardly contain my excitement. I impulsively told her that I loved her, then quickly recovered my wits, apologized and thanked her for the best news of my week. I phoned my sister and told her the good news (I did not tell her that I excitedly told Mabel that I loved her) and asked her if she might know of a family that might care for her until her baby was born and for a year after while she got some training to support herself. She agreed to devote time to it. Come for dinner at mom and dad's Sunday evening and I should have some news. I phoned nurse Rita and explained how this option was developing and to please let Susan know so that she could give it serious consideration.

Thank you, Father in heaven for intervening so wonderfully in this young woman's complicated problems. You, Father, have reminded me again how you are a wonderful God of surprises, a caring God. Thank you for Susan, Dr. Hazelton, Nurse Rita, Mabel and my sister.

CHAPTER 12

Core teaching, #2 "Love of neighbor" (Saturday/Sunday, August 04/05)

Dear friends, you may remember that last Sunday, I talked about loving God. Today, I wish to focus on the second core belief of the Church, that is, the love of one's neighbor. Service, kindness or being helpful are integral parts of loving or serving one's neighbor. Christ at the last supper washed the feet of the apostles. "So, if I, your Lord and Teacher, have washed your feet, you also ought to wash one another's feet. For I have set you an example, that you also should do as I have done for you". In biblical times, washing someone's feet was the work of a servant. Regardless of our state in life, Christians are asked to serve one another. Service can include being helpful to your spouse, your partner, your children, your relatives, your friends, your neighbors and the community both here and afar. The washing of feet implies doing ordinary or menial tasks for those around us. It involves putting their needs ahead of your own. Matthew reminds that when we give a cup of water to anyone in need, it is more than just giving someone a cup of water. We are giving Christ a cup of water. Christ identifies with those in need and associates giving water to those in need as a gift to Him personally. We are interacting with Christ. The story of the Good Samaritan which you have heard so many times, reminds us that we are to care for outsiders or those experiencing economic, social and mental difficulties. Service to our fellow man is our badge of identity or our badge of courage. Family, friends or strangers who are experiencing need cannot not always pick themselves up by their bootstraps but reply on those of us who have an abundance and who are able to help. It is easy to blame those in these situations for making bad decisions or exercising poor judgment. But who are we to judge? God does not judge us and we are not supposed to judge others. He provides the sun and the rain on both the rich and the poor as well as church goers and non-church goers.

Loving one's neighbor means assuming or taking on their issues, their mistakes and their human failings. As St. Paul states so clearly, we are to be kind and helpful. Unfortunately, what is not talked about enough is that loving someone not only changes them or heals them but it changes us and heals us. We become better persons. It broadens us. It makes us bigger human persons.

Think about it. What happens when we help our neighbor put in his crops in the Spring because he has not been well. He feels a debt to you and offers to help you with your chores or getting your crops off in the Fall. This is very familiar to all of you. Kindness begets kindness. Parental love for a child motivates the child to avoid disappointing or upsetting his or her father or mother. Do you remember when someone helped you when you were in a difficult situation years ago? I have such clear memories and also the awareness that we would not be able thank them properly, perhaps because they have died, so we then tried to repay that kindness by being kind to a stranger. Loving someone is calming, healing and a gift to oneself.

CHAPTER 13

Sunday dinner with family.
(Sunday, August 05)

My sister informed me that she was still working on a safe home for Susan. My brother-in-law has a sister Isabella, who is married with two young children in a suitable city in the next province. Her husband, a geologist, works for a mining company and is frequently away. Susan would be good company for them. We are trying to finalize this option. Do you have money for this young woman? Yes, the CWL will cover her financial needs during the pregnancy and for a year after. Wow, nice parishioners, she said. I winked at her and asked her why she was not giving me any credit here. She looked at me and said, "Big brother, sorry, no credit to you. They were probably that way before you arrived".

Father in heaven, creator and ruler of everything. When I look at your sky late at night, the moon, the stars when the town is quiet, I am amazed and thankful that you love and care for us. We are made in your image and likeness and you crown us with glory and honor. You gave us dominion over what you have made such the animals, plants and insects. How wonderful you are!!! Thank you for giving me this parish to work in, the kind parishioners and my family. I pray for Bishop Ben, Pope Francis and world peace.

CHAPTER 14

August visit with Bishop Ben
(Monday, August 06)

The Bishop had asked me to meet with him on Tuesday before lunch in his office. Wonderful, two nights sleeping in my old bed at my parent's home. He began by asking how was I doing getting to know the leaders in the community? After giving Max, his entitled hug and quick ear rub, I gave the Bishop an overview of July's activities, meeting with the key players on each of the parish committees. I was excited to be able to recount my involvement with Susan and the wonderful way the hospital and the CWL came together to help her. We are still working on a safe home in a large city where she can live out her pregnancy and get her life in order. I related about my visit with Rev Mrs. Claire Meadows and her church's financial situation. He agreed that the situation sounded serious. He said that I should leave it with him while he made some phone calls. He asked me about my visit with Mabel Armstrong. I replied that she intimidated me terribly during our first visit. She reminds me of a stern Mother Superior. I left feeling that I would have to work very hard to gain her trust and confidence. Then she came through marvelously for the young girl Susan. I did not mention to him that my response to her generosity was to tell her that loved her before recovering and quickly apologizing. He congratulated me on my excellent beginning. He said, changing the subject, that he wanted me to organize a deanery meeting for the priests in the rural parishes in my locale. Parishes that are within a two-hour driving distance are normally organized into deaneries. Ideally, deaneries meet monthly on church matters as well as provide intellectual and emotional support to the priests who live and work alone. There has not been a meeting for over two years. He said to me, let's choose a Tuesday in mid-September. You host it. There should be six parishes. I will bring sandwiches. Can you make a pot of soup? We will meet from noon to 3:00 pm and create a plan for monthly meetings. I agreed. Later that day, Sis phoned and left a message that Isabella had agreed to welcome Susan into their home during the pregnancy and while she got herself settled. Isabella had agreed to CWL's compensation money and Nurse Rita has agreed to drive Susan to her new home.

Thank you, Father, in heaven for helping to organize these kind events. Thank you for my family, especially my sister. Thank you for Bishop Ben's calm leadership.

CHAPTER 15

My mother's visit
(Wednesday, August 10)

My mother arrived today at 11:00 with lunch and to scout out the living conditions of her fragile but precious "little boy". We had minestrone soup and fresh tomato, mayo and basil on fresh baguette rolls. After lunch and after putting her suitcase in my spare room, I gave her the "cooks tour" of the rectory, the Church and the town including the hospital, the high school, the RCMP office, main street including the grocery store, Tim Hortons and Gregorio's Pizza Parlor that took all of 30 minutes. Arriving back at the rectory, I showed her to the spare bedroom. She requested some nap time but she wanted a more detailed look of the kitchen with stove, frig and laundry facilities later. She was ultimately quite impressed. We then sat down and talked about everything ranging from family, life in this rural community and my support system. She asked if I will be hiring a house-keeper. Not immediately. I need to live on my own and manage on my own. She agreed. I told her that what she could do for me was to teach me how to cook and give me a few good recipes.

Father in Heaven, as I end this day, thank you for everything that happened today especially the company of my mother. Thank you, God, for creating mothers who bring food to their hungry cooking-challenged sons. Please take care of my family and the mothers of the parish and the community.

CHAPTER 16

Phone call with Ed Malone (Friday, August 10)

Later that day, I had a phone call from Ed Malone, publisher of the weekly newspaper, Prairie News. He wanted to come by for an interview for an upcoming edition of his paper. I was taken off guard and asked him why. He persisted; Fred Bartlett and Bill McMillan both members of your parish have alerted him to your enthusiasm and your concern for the parish and the community. They are delighted to have a resident priest. They think you could play a special role in the community; you know, a pair of fresh eyes. By the way, Fred and Bill are in my Monday night poker club. There are eight of us who play for two hours on a $5.00 limit. We have a table set up in my garage. We have a beer and a cigar. No one loses more than $5.00. Once your $5.00 is gone, you play on the house. You may want to join us. They are a good group of guys. I thanked him kindly for the invitation but informed him that Monday is my regular day off and I am often not in the community. Turning this conversation around, I asked him what he thought the parish could do for the community? There was a long silence, he was obviously caught off guard. He began by stating that he was just a quiet newspaperman that was not a particularly religious man. He went to university in Toronto and worked for the Toronto Tribune, a national daily newspaper until his wife, Elaine, a born and bred westerner, convinced him that she needed to breath western air again. So, they agreed to move west and now enjoy what the west had to offer. When he started looking for work, this paper was looking for an editor and they accepted him. The town subsidizes the newspaper and pays him a generous salary. He reads the eastern papers every day. But back to you, what do I call you? I suggested that he call me Cam. OK Cam, what did he have to do to get my consent to this interview? Did he get his story from Fred and Bill? No, I replied. I will make a deal with you. I will consent to your interview if you agree to run occasional articles in your paper on a religious nature. Why, he asked? I told him that the community could benefit from some occasional basic Christian or spiritual teachings. I also told him that I was organizing an inter-denominational study group and we may want to write articles from time to time for publication in his newspaper that could benefit the community. He agreed and asked when could we meet? I told him that I was only available next week Tuesday at 3:00 pm at the rectory, the new mobile home. After he hung up, I wondered what was I getting myself into?

Father in Heaven, thank you for everything you do for me and the opportunities you provide me every day. Thank you for Ed and Elaine Malone, the leaders of our community, the medical staff, the RCMP and families of the community.

CHAPTER 17

Core teaching #3 Forgiveness (Saturday/Sunday, August 11/12)

D ear friends in Christ, the topic of my homily today is forgiveness. When I was in my teen years growing up, I made many foolish mistakes. One such mistake was hiding my report card because it was well below my parent's expectations. Fortunately, they were very forgiving. After I got my learner's license, I foolishly took my mother's car for a ride with my buddies while my parents were away visiting my grandparents. When she returned and found the gas tank on her car was empty, my parents called a family meeting where the three of us, my brother, my sister and I were asked to explain. My brother and sister looked at me accusingly. I eventually confessed. They grounded me for a month but they forgave me as they had done in the past. We forgive because we have been forgiven. Christ has taught that there can be no end to the number of times that we must forgive others. Why, because God our Father loves and continues to forgive us our mistakes. So, without a clear appreciation of how much our Father in heaven loves and forgives us, we will struggle trying to forgive others. The daily examination of conscience is highly recommended as it reminds us of our human-ness and our personal failures as well as our constant need of our Father's loving forgiveness. This awareness will enable us to be more patient and more tolerant with family, friends and associates.

A badge of honor for us followers of Christ is forgiveness. It is the ability to put aside our feelings of hurt, anger and disappointment and give this person a second chance. This can be very hard to do. Forgiveness is important because we live in community with others; a family community including a spouse and children; a work community, social community or a recreational community. Forgiveness gets easier when we realize our humanness, our many mistakes either intentionally or unintentionally. So, because we fail, God forgives us of our mistakes. As God forgives us, we are asked to forgive others. How often? A question asked by Peter, one of the apostles to which Christ responded, seventy time seven. This means that there can be no limit on our forgiveness. In the prayer the Our Father, we ask the Father to forgive us our trespasses or our debts as we forgive others. This is conditional; if I do not forgive, God does not have to forgive us.

Forgiveness is a key part of our mandate to love. Forgiveness is fundamental to our relationship with God. The Psalm 145 states, "The Lord is gracious and merciful, slow to anger and abounding in steadfast love. The Lord is good to all and his compassion is over all that he has made. The Lord is faithful in all his words and gracious in all his deeds. The Lord upholds all who are falling, and raises up all who are burdened." So, because God has first forgiven us, we must forgive others.

Why is it so hard to forgive others? Perhaps, we were made to look bad or were embarrassed. We also know however that these mistakes by others are sometimes unintended. So, we need to practice keeping our ego in check and giving others the benefit of the doubt.

Father in heaven help me to give my parishioners, family and friends the benefit of the doubt when I feel slighted, ignored or criticized. Thank you for your constant forgiveness of my many past mistakes, my selfishness and my neglect of those who love me.

CHAPTER 18

Visit from Father Joe from the Benedictine Monastery, (Tuesday, August 14)

F ather Joe had phoned me last week to say that he was going to be visiting a sick uncle in my vicinity and could he come by for a visit? I assured him that I had a comfortable spare bedroom, lots of frozen dinners courtesy of my mother and a very good pizza parlor down the street. He arrived after lunch today wearing his black tunic and cowl. He asked if he could nap before we visit? Of course, I said. At 3:00 PM he appeared looking very refreshed in jeans and a t-shirt. He accepted a cup of my strong coffee and asked me to fill him in on what has happened since my ordination 14 months ago. I told him about my pleasant first year with Fr. Mike Thomas as his assistant in a city parish. I told him about my continuing concern that so many people are abandoning the church and my visits with Joe and Mary. But when I discussed these ideas with Fr. Mike, he agreed but was uncomfortable about putting such ideas into practice. He would find it too stressful at his age. Fr. Mike also advised me to be careful about implementing change in my first year on my own as a parish priest. I arrived in this parish in early July and am still getting my feet wet. We talked about the application of Benedictine spirituality, the oldest Christian monastic practice, to my life as a priest. He unequivocally stated that obedience (to your Bishop and the Church), stability (the being comfortable where you are without needing to escape) and hospitality were applicable to your life. He went on to say that the lesson of Christ the good shepherd was probably equally appropriate here. He reminded me that Christ was willing to leave the ninety-nine in the wilderness and go in search of the sheep that was lost until he finds it. This is a very powerful analogy for your practice in this parish. I told him about my conversation with the Bishop who said that he could not give me permission but would give me forgiveness for my pastoral indiscretions. Joe laughed and asked me what I thought of his response. I stated that it was a good sign that he could be tolerant when required. He also, in so many words, gave me permission to follow my conscience when dealing with a current church practice that I felt was in transition and that I did not fully agree with, provided they were based on good theological reasons. Then Joe went on to say that their alcoholic and drug rehab programs were not doing well. The level of participants was well down from the past. He suspects that there are newer treatment facilities opening up that do not require the participants to work or contribute. While the work was physically hard when I was at the Abbey, once I did a few days' work, my body adjusted. Later, we picked up a couple of Gregorio's famous pizzas and he purchased some Corona beer and we chatted into the night about the Vatican, our head office, the history of the Benedictines, the role of the Abbot as a symbol of mercy and justice and our respective families. He heard my confession and my current guilt for my failure to care for Wendy as she deserved during her final days and for my persistent guilt for the alcohol-induced one-night stands following her death. Before retiring, we both agreed on how restorative our visit was. We concelebrated mass next morning and he left after breakfast.

Father in heaven, have mercy on me for you are good and forgiving, full of mercy to all who call to you. Thank you.

CHAPTER 19

Interview with Ed Malone
(Thursday, August 16)

At 9:30 am sharp, Ed arrived at my door with tape recorder in hand. I offered him some fresh coffee. Writers and newspaper folks like him, he volunteered, thrive on a daily intake of gallons of strong black coffee. I offered toast which he accepted but only with peanut butter and strawberry jam. He certainly knew how to quickly make himself feel at home. So, while he organized himself at my kitchen table close to an electrical outlet, I made him toast with peanut butter and jam. As we sat down, I asked him to tell me a little about himself. He was raised in a small town called Goderich located in western Ontario, near London. He went to journalism school at Ryerson in Toronto and joined the Toronto Tribune, one of Canada's national newspapers. He met his wife Elaine, a nurse in a bar one night. It was love at first sight. They married within 2 months and found a basement suite in Little Italy, a proud Italian community in the heart of Toronto. She worked in a street clinic with homeless people. They were busy and loved the street life, the shops and restaurants in their adopted Italian community. After 10 years of loving life in Toronto, Elaine got up one morning and said it was time to move back to the prairies and breathe clean air again. She was born and raised a prairie girl growing up in big sky country. This editor's job was vacant and I jumped at it. Elaine's nursing background enabled her to work anywhere. They have been in this community for 12 years and love it. OK, he said, now it is your turn. Tell me briefly where you grew up, your marriage and your life as a celibate priest.

I grew up in the city, 45 minutes from here. I am so tired

of telling my story; Ed, I had a very normal life growing in the city. lots of sports, I was a middle child with an older brother who works with my dad in the building supplies trade and have a younger sister who is a high school teacher. Both are married and have children. We were raised Catholic; our parents practiced a quiet faith, nothing ostentatious or fancy. They were good neighbors, kind to family and friends alike. I met Wendy in high school and we became sweethearts. We both studied social work at UBC and got married during our university years. We had a wonderful marriage and we worked hard. She was a marriage counselor and I worked in the development and the construction of affordable housing. At 35, Wendy was sadly diagnosed with an aggressive form of ALS that was untreatable. After four years of declining health, she chose to die with dignity and spare us the pain of her painful and agonizing death. She asked us to take her to the United States where she had a doctor assisted death. I know you are going to ask if Catholics are allowed to have a doctor assisted death. No, they are not. Wendy, however, had a lot of problems with the Church because of the horrible way it treats women, divorced Catholics and the LGBTQ community. These people were her clients and she fought for them, that is until she became too ill. After Wendy died, I was a lost soul, drank a lot to deal with the loss of her and fortunately ended up in an alcoholic treatment program run by the Benedictines. I was impressed with the monks and their 1500-year-old spirituality so I went back to university to study philosophy and eventually theology. So, it was only in my late 30s that I began to consider this life.

Do I miss the intimacy and the affection of Wendy? Yes, of course, I do. I dream of her regularly, sometimes it is dream that I did not care for her well enough in her final days. She will be a significant part of my entire life. But I have also been introduced to what is known as a contemplative way of life, practiced by all major religions. It supports one to live a very focused and goal-oriented life-style that I need. I am also quite close to my parents, my brother and sister, their spouses and their children who treat me well and give me lots of hugs. I usually get home most Sunday evenings for a family meal. While I have considerable emotional support, I still feel vulnerable for the companionship of a wife. It is normal to experience that. But as I mentioned previously, I have a fulfilling inner spiritual life that helps me to stay content and focused. When I am feeling emotionally vulnerable, I phone my sister. She is a wonderful listener.

Now he wanted to know if I will be preaching on a podium in the public square soon. I said no. I think our actions speak louder than words. He thanked me for this charming visit, the toast and coffee. He will prepare an article and gave me assurance that I could review it before it is published.

Father in heaven, thank you for Ed. Keep him and Elaine in your love and guide them along their life's journey. I love the way he uses his weekly newspaper as a community building resource.

CHAPTER 20

Core teaching #4, "God's ways are not our ways" (Saturday/ Sunday, August 18/19)

Dear friends, who is this God of love, this God of surprises? In Matthew's gospel, chapter 20, verses 1-16, there is a parable called workers in the vineyard. A landowner hires workers for his vineyard beginning at dawn. The workers agree to the usual daily wage. He hires more workers at nine o'clock, at noon, at three o'clock and at five o'clock, all agreeing to the usual daily wage. When it is evening, he summons all these workers and gives them their pay. They all received the same amount of money even those who arrived at five o'clock. When the first workers learned what was happening, they complained to the landowner as they thought that they should have received more than the others after working in the heat for the whole day. The landowner replied that they were paid the amount that they had agreed to accept.

I have never understood this parable as it smacks of unfairness and even injustice. Why is God carrying on in this way? When I read a professional commentary of this parable, the landowner represents God. God's generosity is not merited but is freely lavished on those most in need. In God's world, all are treated equally and loved equally. God does not give us what we deserve in terms of forgiving our wrongdoings or even in rewarding our good deeds. The story of Dismas, the good thief who died on the cross with Jesus is informative. After some sort of criminal activity not explained, he made a death bed confession to Jesus and was assured a heavenly reward. This is the basis for a priest's attendance when someone is dying.

In Isaiah, an Old Testament prophet, chapter 55, verse 8, he speaks for God. "For my thoughts are not your thoughts, nor are your ways, my ways, says the Lord. For as the heavens are higher than the earth, so are my ways higher than your ways and my thoughts than your thoughts."

Sometimes, it is hard to understand what God is asking of us. My deceased wife Wendy, was a really good person. She dedicated herself to disadvantaged women and advocated for them. In spite of that, ALS struck her down in the prime of her life. I was devastated and struggled to understand our life and then my life. I frequently asked, "Why me?" My conclusion was that there are many things in life that do not make sense and are totally devoid of rationality. After a few months, it occurred to me, "Why not me?" Am I so privileged that I am entitled to a life without conflict, sadness and suffering? I am not.

Father in heaven, thank you for everything you do for me. Help me to see life from your perspective and not get bent out of shape when things go sideways in my life. Give me the courage to keep loving you and those around me.

CHAPTER 21

Core teaching #5, "disturbing emotions" (Saturday/ Sunday, August 25/26)

Dear friends, have you ever been driving down a street slowly while you looked carefully for an address without realizing that traffic had jammed up behind you? Out of the blue, the person behind you leans on the horn, scares the devil out of you and raises his hands as if to say what is wrong with you. You immediately pull over and wave an apology but the driver has already sped off annoyed. The driver's reaction is called having disturbing emotions. Having these negative feelings can affect your other relationships unless you are able dig beneath the surface of these behaviors and discover what caused your reaction. In the example of the driver, he perhaps became annoyed with the slowness of the traffic. He probably was on his way to pick up his son from school and he was late. Perhaps he did not plan on slow traffic. He is now angry and his son will unknowingly experience his anger without knowing why. Or the father could have realized what he was experiencing and remained calm, apologized to his son for being late and gone for an ice cream cone.

Another example, suppose you are at a social event and a person whom you thought was a good friend, snubs you resulting in you feeling surprised, bewildered and perhaps hurt. What do these disturbing emotions tell us about ourselves? In the case of the social snub, we thought that we had made a good friend. Good friends do not treat each other this way. I may have made an incorrect assumption about our relationship and the other person does not share my perception. The person may have had a bad day and did not realize the significance that her avoidance behavior would have on me.

Regardless, maybe we are taking ourselves too seriously. We need to practice tolerance and forgiveness of this person. It also means trying to create space between this event and ourselves. How do we improve our ability to be more tolerant and forgiving? One suggestion is through finding time alone and quiet reflection. This can help us to become more conscious of our unique challenges and prepare ourselves to act differently day to day.

Takeaways:

1. Allow such feelings to surface but have a good look at them. Let them teach you;
2. Talk out your angry feelings no matter how small they are. This can prevent them from becoming bigger problems;
3. There can be just anger;
4. Be careful of generalizing your anger from a small thing to a large thing;
5. Anger can be a reflection of one's ego; and
6. According to Buddhists, enlightenment is the habitual state of imperturbable calm.

CHAPTER 22

CWL meeting (Thursday, August 30)

There were seven of us at this meeting; Mabel Armstrong as chair, Hilary Bartlett, Ann McCaffrey, Liz McMillan, Judy Truman, Ruth Hanson and me. After introductions, I opened the meeting with all of us reciting the Lord's prayer. Mabel asked Ruth to take minutes of the meeting and turned the meeting over to me. But as I was not comfortable with that, I asked her to please lead the meeting. Mabel reported that she had received some replies to letters that they had mailed to Federal politicians concerning their lax attitude on permitting abortions. She read the first response, "Thank you to the Catholic Women's League for your letter. You are preaching to the choir if I may use one of your religious analogies. No one in our caucus believes in abortion but a majority of the electorate do. I wished that I had a better answer for you. Thank you for taking the time to write to us". Letter #2, "Thank you ladies of the CWL for your letter. Our party opposes abortion as you do but women need a safe, protective environment to work through an unwanted pregnancy. Our research has shown that most of those women seeking an abortion are of low income. Improving their educational and employment skills could be something you could focus on rather than banning abortions. Could you please focus your efforts on such a solution rather than attacking these poor young victims? Thank you." Letter #3, "Thank you for your letter. Regardless of how upsetting this is for you and your organization, abortions unfortunately are allowed and are not criminal acts. We are sorry". Mabel very sternly asked me if I have ever preached a sermon on the evils of abortion. I said no, not yet. I explained that I share the second respondent's point of view that the need for an abortion is tied up with poverty and with those who are experiencing multiple social problems in their lives. Telling someone who is both poor and with an unwanted pregnancy not to have an abortion, seems to me to be re-victimizing them. I also do not think that we as Church should tell other people how to live or impose our values on them. I then related the story of Susan and her unwanted pregnancy and how significant the CWL's financial and supportive intervention was. Susan has moved to an anonymous location where she is now living with a young mother with two pre-school children while she is upgrading her employment skills. I thanked them for turning this young woman's life around and financing the next year and a half of her life. I reminded them that the story of Susan and the CWL's support for her is worth more than twenty sermons on the evils of abortion. Mabel then turned the meeting over to me. Liz, another stern looking hawk, asked me how the Church reacted to your wife's assisted death? I took a deep breath and realized that this was going to be a meeting to remember. I told them that Wendy, my deceased wife had a lot of disagreements with Catholicism. She was a therapist who was very supportive of women particularly those that were in abusive relationships. She encouraged Catholic women in abusive relationships to leave their husbands which was contrary to the advice of many priests. She thought that the church's attitude to women in general was horrible and dismissive and, in the end, she decided to follow her conscience on dealing with her ravaging ALS disease. She felt that dying on her own terms and while she had control over her faculties was better not just for her but for those of us she left behind, namely me, her parents and her siblings. She was prepared to go it alone. I questioned the difference between Wendy's choosing 8 milligrams of secobarbital to end her life in dignity and the current medical practice of using increasing doses of morphine for patients in palliative care that results in their slow death. I have seen dementia patients warehoused in long term care centres who can neither feed themselves nor clean themselves waiting for death. Liz, not letting me off the hook, asked if she was buried in the church, I replied no, she was not. Liz continued, did you try to discourage your wife from choosing assisted suicide? Now I felt that I too was on trial. My role, I thought at the time, was only to support her in every way possible. No, I did not try to discourage her. She had carefully analyzed all the options and did not ask for my advice. Liz continued, are you pro-life? Yes, very much so. Others members in the meeting were very supportive, expressing how painful this must have been for me and her family. This discussion left a pall over the meeting. I quickly changed the subject and asked if they felt that a Catholic could still be considered still a good Catholic if they did not believe in all the teachings of the church such as assisted dying? Pope Francis hinted that such was possible when he stated that a person's spiritual development was much like our intellectual or psychological development. Spiritual maturity is slow and develops over a lifetime but sometimes in life we take steps backwards as we struggle to understand life's challenges and dilemmas. Wendy's death for example, was initially very bewildering for me. Why was this bad thing happening to Wendy, who was such a good person? I had to learn to let feelings and confusion go and trust in God for an answer. To change the subject again, I then I inquired about how the CWL raised its money. There was a prolonged silence while they all looked uncomfortably at one another. Finally, Mabel explained that this was their secret. The community runs a weekend casino in the city annually and makes approximately $50,000.00. This money is doled out to be used for charitable or non-profit causes. The CWL gets a small amount for such things as Christmas hampers and supporting people like Susan. Is this endeavor listed as a St. Francis event? No, it is community initiative called The Families Helping Families Association. The parish had heard that some dioceses are opposed to using casinos to raise funds. Furthermore, operating on our own without the benefit of consistent parish priest, we have learned that we function quite well operating on our own. Changing the subject again, I inquired if there were women on the parish council. Mabel said no. Did you think there should be women on the council? They were unanimous in responding yes. I thanked them. Changing the subject again, I then explained how important relationships are in our Catholic beliefs and practices and especially marital relationships. When I introduced myself to Mabel in August, I asked her if we could spend a few minutes at this meeting talking about what women want in a marriage relationship. I told them that I would be asking the men's club the same question, of wanting to share the information with both groups and ultimately with the permission of both groups, writing an article for the weekly newspaper. I advised them that Ed Malone has agreed to find me space. After they agreed, I gave each of them pen and paper for their answers. I then organized a flip chart where I could write their answers for all to see. I assured them that their responses would remain confidential and anonymous. So, each of them made some notes that I have summarized as follows. Could husbands: 1. Take more initiatives in the kitchen and with household chores; 2. Be less dominant in the family and quit acting as if they have all the answers; 3. Brush your teeth more; 4. Change your clothes more frequently; 5. Quit smoking; 6. Watch less sports on TV; 7. Be more companionable and to do the things that only women enjoy; 8. Be less pre-occupied with sex and be more affectionate; 9. Give more hugs. 10. Give us foot rubs and back rubs without expecting sex in return. 11. Read more and share what you read with us. 12. Give us a regular day off without having to prepare meals or worry about child care. 13. Let us be the boss once in a while. Wow!!! I was very impressed with their responses. I explained that the next step was to have the list typed up for the next month's meeting. I thanked them for their support and cooperation. They also gave me permission to share their suggestions with the members of the men's club and in the local newspaper. In closing I told them how much I admired their Catholic practice. It takes a strong faith and a lot of determination to remain a committed practicing Catholic today.

Father in heaven, thank you for all your help and wise counsel today with the CWL. Help me to be patient with their beliefs and values. Keep them close to you and safe.

CHAPTER 23

Article for the Prairie News Saturday, (Friday, August 31)

Inter-Denominational matters

All inter-denominational religious leaders of our community are cordially invited to an introductory meeting on Thursday, September 12 at the Anglican Church Manse to begin at 11:00 am. Please bring your lunch and coffee will be served. RSVP. Rev. Claire Meadows, 454-6090.

I phoned Ed and thanked him for the article in the paper. He asked how many people I was expecting? I said that I had no idea but we would not turn anyone away.

Father in heaven, thank you for Ed Malone. Keep him and Elaine close to you and safe in your love. Thank you for the article in the local newspaper.

CHAPTER 24

Core teaching #6 "Our God of second chances (Saturday/ Sunday, September 01/02)

God our father is a God of second chances. What does this mean? The Gospels are filled with stories of second chances for example, the prodigal son. You will recall how he foolishly spent his inheritance in fast living and decided to come home hoping to work for his father and brother in a lowly position on their farm. His worried father sensing that all was not right, was waiting in anticipation of his return and gladly welcomed him home in spite of the displeasure of his older son. Peter, the apostle, who betrayed Christ during his suffering and death, was given a second chance to become the leader of the early church and its first pope. Second chances result from a failure to do something. However, after admitting your failure, you are forgiven and the relationship is restored. For some, forgiveness is very difficult and the relationship remains broken. For others, it is easier. Why is it easier for some to forgive? One reason is that they have made mistakes and experienced forgiveness. Mercy and forgiveness are very closely connected. Matthew's Gospel includes mercy as one of the beatitudes, "Blessed are the merciful, for they shall obtain mercy." Mercy is based on our own self-awareness of our humanness, our human frailty and our past mistakes. Mercy also includes an appreciation of how much God has been merciful to us day in and day out. God our Father loves as we are and wants a relationship with us. Our Father in heaven is as the Psalmist says, "The Lord is gracious and merciful, slow to anger and abounding in steadfast love.

The Lord is good to all and his compassion is over all that he has made."

Paul of Tarsus is another example. He, as a young adult, was a dedicated Pharisee and persecuted the early Christians until he had a miraculous conversion. He became the apostle that welcomed non-Jewish converts into the church. He also wrote many epistles that form part of the New Testament. Second chances abound in both the Old and New Testaments.

Father in heaven, preaching on second chances gives me great pleasure.

CHAPTER 25

Reflection time (Monday, September 03)

Nothing special happened; breakfast with mother who chatted my ear off about proper dietary practices. She also filled me in on how much fun the four grandchildren have become. I had lunch with Fr. Mike and dinner with Sis, Trevor, Pat and Patty.

God our loving Father, thank you for my parents, my siblings, my grandchildren and my parishioners. Please keep them safe and in your love.

CHAPTER 26

Scripture Course: Adam and Eve (Tuesday, September 04)

Summary of class notes:

- The story of creation and Adam and Eve is found in the Book of Genesis, chapters 1 to 3;
- According to my instructors, there is no historical basis for the story of creation and the first eleven books of the Bible. In spite of all the archaeological work, there is no supportive evidence that any of the key people in these stories have ever lived;
- My instructors suggest that the first eleven books were written between 1200 and 400 B.C.E.;
- The writers of Genesis present a God as Father who speaks everything into existence. His word is a creative force;
- He brings all orders of being into existence in sequence like an architect constructing an apartment or an office building;
- He constructs a physical environment for all forms of life culminating in humankind;
- He takes a piece of clay and breathes human life into it;
- Humans are created in the image and the likeness of God. Humans act like him when procreating, when developing order and harmony in the world and when exercising care for the earth/environment;
- Male and female together, not separately, bear the image and likeness of God. They are complimentary;

- He wants to be near to us. He desires an intimacy and closeness with us. God created with great care and attention;
- He walks in the garden in the cool of the evening after seemingly a busy day of creation. He seeks out Adam and Eve for company and companionship. They have disobeyed and had eaten the forbidden fruit. They avoid him;
- In spite of their disobedience, God is kind and helpful by sowing leather garments to cover their nakedness;
- In spite of his desire for intimacy with the first members of the human family, there is tension in the relationship. As he approaches, they withdraw;
- Even though Adam and Eve enjoyed the perfect world of the Garden of Eden and were able to be face to face with God, it seems that they made mistakes by not accepting their limits. Their sin was not only a personal act of rebellion, but as the Church teaches, their act of rebellion had long term consequences for us all.

The writer of Adam and Eve's story provides the reader with few details explaining what happened, so to flesh out their story, this is what I imagined the fuller picture might be. Cain and his younger brother Seth are now two old men, both retired and like most old men, they reminisce about the early days of the family, the good old days. They are sitting around a fire and admiring the full moon and chatting:

Seth: Cain, what caused you to kill our brother Abel?
Cain: Abel was arrogant and very competitive. He thought that he was so much better than me. So, one day, in a fit of rage I killed him. There has not been one day since that I have not regretted what I did.
Seth: Did Adam forgive you?

Cain: Yes, both parents forgave me. They first learned forgiveness from God, who helped them to cloth themselves and to survive outside the Garden of Eden. They had to learn to forgive themselves too. They believed that forgiveness was a basic part of living in a family.

Seth: Why did our parents disobey the Lord? They had everything they wanted in the garden.

Cain: That is a tough question. I am not even sure that they themselves know. My guess is that they wanted more than they had. Isn't there an expression, "A person's reach should exceed his/her grasp." We take risks sometimes without knowing what the consequences are. The first lady also had a sweet tooth for apples and Adam always wanted to please Eve. He always said that he loved her more than she loved him. You know the rule, "Happy wife means happy life".

Cain looked at the moon and said, "Seth, look at that beautiful moon. Do you think we will ever travel to the moon?

Seth: Good question! What an interesting idea.

My takeaways: we are all flawed persons; needing to be forgiven and accommodated. If I were in Adam and Eve's shoes, would I have acted any differently? Consistently doing what is right can be a challenge and a struggle. I too, have moments when I avoid my relationship with the Father, the God of love. Thank you, Father, in heaven for all you do for me.

CHAPTER 27

Meet the Bishop
(Wednesday, September 05)

I had lunch with the Bishop and two colleagues at the Cathedral today and then we went back to his office for my monthly meeting. After having given Max a cuddle and his entitled ear rubs, I outlined my activities during August and in particular the September CWL meeting where they inquired about my wife's assisted dying. I explained in great detail that this was my wife's choice. He said nothing in response. They even asked me if I was pro-life. Of course, I replied in the affirmative. I also told him about their responses to my question about what do women want in marriage. He listened very carefully and asked what was my purpose in this question. I explained promoting good marriage relationships has many spiritual and psychological benefits. I continued giving him an overview of my upcoming September meetings. He had one question; how is the planning for the Deanery meeting progressing? I reminded him that we have scheduled Thursday, September 20 for this meeting. I had talked to Margaret, your secretary and she had confirmed that you were available on that day. He thanked me for all that I do. Driving away, I felt that Bishop Ben was concerned today about having assigned me too soon to work alone and now forced to forgive me for a lot of things.

Father in heaven, thank you for Bishop Ben, Max and Margaret.

CHAPTER 28

Men's group meeting
(Thursday, September 06)

O ur meeting began at 7:30 pm in the rectory boardroom. Present were Fred Bartlett, Bill McMillan, Tom McCaffrey, Jim Truman, Nick Hanson and me. Ned Armstrong, Mabel's husband was out of town. Looking around the room, it occurred to me that there seems to be a very small core of committed Catholics keeping this parish functioning. After introductions, Bill turned to me to take over the meeting: I thanked them for coming to this meeting. I briefly presented an overview of my life, my marriage, my work, Wendy's work with women particularly in abusive relationships, her illness and her choice of ending her life on her own terms, my drinking, my days with the Benedictines and being introduced to a spiritual life, my going back to school, studying philosophy and theology, ordination and working with Fr. Mike last year. Bill wanted to know what motivated me to become a priest. After my university education in social work, I leaned toward service work, namely the development of affordable housing and women's emergency shelters. After I lost my wife, I realized that life was short, and we are on this earth for a brief time so I should use my talents and skills to the best that I can. The priesthood seemed one avenue where I combine my newly found life with God, my social work education and my work experience.

Bill introduced his next question by describing it as awkward and then asked what my experience was like trying to blend marriage and the priesthood. I replied that I am very happy as a priest, but my outlook has been framed by my marriage to Wendy. Even though I am a priest, I think of her every day.

As you know, we were high school sweethearts. Do I miss the love of a wife? Yes, Wendy and I had a wonderful life for ten years. She was a gift. To be loved by her, in my opinion, was something very special. Then her ALS took over and our focus was on keeping her as comfortable as possible. Losing Wendy whom I loved and depended upon, bent me out of shape. I still love her and think of her every day. I was devastated when she died and then drank six months of my life away to cope with the loss. The Benedictines gave me a second chance. My parents, siblings and grandchildren live in the city and have been a big emotional support to me. I try to make the family dinners on Sunday nights. During my rehabilitation from alcoholism at the monastery, I learned about having an active daily spiritual relationship with God and the experience of God's love and forgiveness as a wonderful source of inspiration to me even to this day. I have discovered that my relationship with God as Father helps me to compensate for what I do not have. I have been told however, that the attractiveness of sex never diminishes even as we age.

Next question: do I attend Alcoholic Anonymous meetings? I was getting very uncomfortable with these personal questions. Do you mean that if I had a drink, would I be a problem drinker? No, I am not an alcoholic. I now enjoy an occasional beer or glass of wine.

Next question, is the Church opposed to pre-marital sex? I explained that it seems that our society seems to becoming more accepting of pre-marital sex with many young people living together before being married. I guess it is a stage in learning how to live in an intimate relationship. When you compare pre-marital sex to other evils in our society such the lack of protection of young girls in the sex trade business, drug overdose issues, poverty and homelessness, I personally do not think this is as big a problem as the Church has made of it I do not spend a lot of time on it, nor do I believe that many priests do at least the ones that I know. If a parent were to express a worry about the sexual activities of their son or daughter, I would suggest that they provide their son or daughter with a generous supply of condoms. There appears to be a shift in society to be more accepting of certain individual rights such as pre-marital sex, divorce, assisted dying and same-sex marriages and abortion except for the CWL (bad joke). Studies and surveys confirm that same sex couples, both men and women, who adopt children, are known to raise very sensitive and well-behaved children. There are some rumors held by some senior officials in the Vatican that the Catholic Church is 200 years behind the times on sexual matters. Ultimately, we each have to educate our consciences by carefully looking at the situation, getting advice from family, friends and professionals and then having the courage to admit when we were wrong. We should learn from the experience.

What about adultery? Is it still as bad as ever?

Yes, it is. It is, in my opinion, poaching on someone's vulnerable marital partner. It can cause considerable unnecessary inter-generational damage. Don't expect changes on this matter.

I then asked the group how the parish or how the men's group could contribute to our community in a meaningful way. This question drew a lot of blank stares and a poor response, so I suggested that we save this matter next month. I asked Bill in the meantime to ask the Town Manager if there was something the men's group could do for the town.

My last question was: what do men want in marriage? I pointed out that I had asked the members of the CWL the same question and received some very thoughtful answers. Tell us, they responded. I told them that I had the CWL ladies permission to share what they talked about but first let's get your responses. Like I did with the CWL, I passed out pen and paper to each of them and prepared my flip chart to record their answers. I assured them that their responses would be confidential. Their responses were summarized as follows: 1. Men generally do not socialize as easily as women, so they need to have time to socialize over a drink with a buddy or with a group of guys; 2. Wives should be more patient with husbands as they struggle to learn to contribute to the home. They should remember that the fathers of the men you married were raised on farms and small towns and where they have traditionally been relegated to the garage, the barn and the fields, whereas the wife to the house, cooking and raising the children. 3. Tell your husband that you love them more. Daily words and hugs are important. 4. Please give us emotional space particularly after an argument. 5. Wives should initiate sex instead of always leaving it up to the husband. 6. Men want to be heard. 7. Men need to be praised, respected and appreciated. 8. Men need to be touched, kissed and hugged. Then I presented what the CWL ladies identified as important in marriage. I reported that I would have both lists typed up for next month's meeting. I thanked them for their questions and marriage suggestions. As this meeting had extended beyond their regular closing time, the group left quickly.

Father in heaven, thank you for a very productive meeting and another wonderful day. Please keep my family and the families of the parish close to your heart. Help all of us to love you more each day and to love those we are responsible for.

CHAPTER 29

Preach on Gratitude (Saturday/Sunday, September 08/09)

My topic today is gratitude. It rates highly in the hierarchy of virtues with love and mercy/forgiveness. It is defined as an awareness of how fortunate and blessed we are with our lives as they are. It can also mean thankfulness for what we have without the need to seek or acquire more. Gratitude can also mean that we do not take things for granted. It is known to turn what we have into abundance. There are benefits to the experience of gratitude; gratitude can enhance the law of attraction and improves our relationships; those with gratitude can be good friends and companions. Gratitude helps one sleep better. It even known to rewire one's brain.

What is the connection of gratitude and the person experiencing difficult times such as sickness, worry and fear? Is there a place for gratitude? Assuredly, sickness, worry and fear can bring a person down to the depths of depression and immobilize us. Friendship means that we reach out to them while they struggle with these personal issues. In time however, we hope they will find the strength to work with the problem by seeking professional advice and consulting family and friends. These struggles can broaden us intellectually and emotionally. Buddhists believe that difficult times and limitations can be opportunities for improvement. They teach that we should be grateful for difficult times as they build strength and character. Our mistakes teach us valuable lessons. The famous Helen Keller, who grew up both blind and deaf is quoted as saying, "I cried because I had no shoes until I met a man who had no feet." St. Teresa of Calcutta is quoted as saying, "Some people come in your life as blessings. Some come in your life as lessons." Very thought-provoking. Gratitude helps us to look at life with perspective.

Why should we be grateful? Our crops look exceptional and our gardens have benefitted from generous rains; we are well served by a medical system with a local hospital including doctors and nurses; we have a wonderful school system with low student-teacher ratios and with well loved and respected teachers; we have a local RCMP detachment with two officers in our community to keep us safe and regularly put themselves in harm's way to keep us safe and we have a local newspaper, keeping us informed on activities in our community.

What is God's role in these benefits? Reviewing my notes on Genesis, we extend God's creative work when we responsibly manage our environment such as gardens, farms and public spaces. Perhaps, we as a parish can show our gratitude by contributing more to our community. I suspect there are numerous tasks that we could assume that would make our town a more desirable place to live. To that end, can each of us take the initiative of asking our friends the doctors, the police, the town administration and the school staff how we as a parish can contribute to the betterment of the community.

Father in heaven, I thank you, I praise you and I adore you for all your gifts. Bless the Lord, O my soul and all that is within me, bless his holy name. Praise the Lord, O my soul and do not forget all his benefits. Amen.

CHAPTER 30

Scripture course Noah, (Tuesday, September 11)

Summary of class notes:

1. The next big story after the story of creation and Adam and Eve, is Noah and the Ark. It is found in the Book of Genesis, chapters 6 to 9, verses 1-17;
2. God the Father saw that the hearts and behaviors of his people had turned to wickedness and had corrupted the earth. He was very disappointed in what he had created.

3. God the Father decided to send a major flood to destroy all of life on earth and start over.
4. He found Noah, described as righteous and blameless. "He walked with God". So, God disclosed his plan to Noah and asked him to build an Ark. God provided Noah with detailed instructions as to size and materials of this Ark that must save every remnant of all life forms on earth.
5. God the Father wanted two of every animal and bird, a male and female. Noah must load food for everyone and everything. God ordered Noah to load his family, animals and birds into the Ark.
6. It rained for 40 days and 40 nights. Water soon covered the earth. Life on earth was destroyed.
7. Sometime later, after the water receded, Noah built an alter to acknowledge his dependence on God and the former good relationship between God and mankind was re-established.
8. God showed compassion with humans and overcame his anger and regret. God made a covenant with Noah pledging never to destroy life again and used a rainbow as a sign of his covenant with Noah.

This is my version of this story with all due respects to the comedic satire of Bill Cosby:

God: Noah, this is God. Put your saw down and listen. I want you to build an ark.
Noah: What's an ark?
God: A big boat.
Noah: Why?
God: I am very unhappy with mankind. They have turned to evil things. I want to destroy all life in the world and start over. I am going to make it rain for 40 days and 40 nights and flood everything. Only life on the ark will be saved. I will

save you, your family, one male and female of every animal and bird species. But this is a secret plan.

Noah: Please get someone else. I am very busy. I have no time for building fancy arks.

God: Noah, how long can you tread water?

Noah: All right then. How big is the ark supposed to be?

God: The measurements are 300 cubits in length, 50 cubits wide and 30 cubits in height. Make rooms in the ark and cover it inside and out with pitch. Make a roof, one cubit above. Make a door on each of the three floors of the ark.

Noah: Wow, that is a big ark. How long do I have to build it?

God: 30 days.

Noah: What are my neighbors going to think?

God: Do not concern yourself with what they say or think.

Noah: I will need a development and building permit and the Planning Department will want to know what is going on. 30 days is not long enough. You know how slow City Hall is in approving development permits.

God: Do not worry about approvals from the Planning Department. I will deal with them.

A few days pass.

God: Noah, are you finished?

Noah: The neighbors are starting to ask questions of my wife. They think that I am crazy and want to put me away. Can you fix that too?

God: Yes, I will fix that too. Done. Hurray up. You are behind schedule.

Noah: God, the Planning Department wants to send their building inspectors to ensure that the ark is properly waterproofed. Can you fix that too?

God: You bet. Done. You have a week left. Remember you need food and treats for yourselves, the animals and birds for 40 days and 40 nights. When are you loading up?

Noah: Finding all these animals and birds is becoming more difficult. I need your help with them.

God: OK. Done.

God and Noah made the deadline and the occupants on the ark were saved to live another day.

Father in heaven, help me to daily walk with you as Noah did.

CHAPTER 31

Update on Susan
(Thursday, September 13)

Nurse Rita called me to tell me about Susan. They have been exchanging weekly letters and Susan is doing well. The pregnancy is progressing well and Susan has signed up to take a legal training assistance course. Thank you again CWL. Father in heaven please care for the depressed, the sad, the lonely and those that mourn.

CHAPTER 32

Meeting of my Protestant colleagues and Homily prep at Bill's home (Thursday, September 13)

Our first inter-denominational meeting was a special event. We met at Claire's home. There were seven of us: Claire Meadows (Anglican), Ed Malone (Editor of Prairie News), Ron Keating (lay Buddhist practitioner), Lay minister Helen Jones, (United Church), Part-time lay minister Matt Johnson, (Baptist Church) Peter Smith (just curious) and me. After introductions, we chatted over our lunch and talked about what we could do together. Suggestions ranged from prayer or meditating together; selecting a book that we could discuss together; becoming a support group; presentations on one another's beliefs would be valuable; community service programs for teens such as a clean water initiative in Mexico or reducing plastics, wilderness survival camps and a community appreciation night could be a goal too. After debating these options, we agreed to jointly put on an evening to acknowledge our appreciation event for the service providers in the town, namely doctors, nurses, hospital staff, teachers, RCMP officers, public library staff, Town administration and members of the Town Council. Ed said that he would coordinate the event through the newspaper. We agreed to hold this evening in late October. I asked that we delay a formal announcement of our plans until we have run it past our respective parishes. I cannot imagine the Bishop as being opposed to this idea.

Later this evening, I joined Bill and Liz McMillan at their home with their two children, Joe (10 years) and Sara (7 years) and their dog, a 2-year-old Labrador retriever named Tom. I reminded them the purpose of my visit to request some help in preparing my Sunday homily as well as to get to know them. I informed them that my subject was love; loving God and loving our neighbor. At my request, Bill red St. Paul's description of love in first Corinthians, that would be one of the readings. Liz began by saying that loving some people was easy, like Bill or the kids but loving others can be very challenging especially if it appears that they do not want your love. Bill said that in his business, he has to be kind and considerate to everyone regardless of how well they respond and has to give them the benefit of the doubt. He finds that chatting up a potential customer can warm them up. I asked Joe and Sarah if they had any thoughts. Joe stated that when he played baseball with his friends, sometimes they cheated. Was he supposed to love a cheater? Sarah said that sometimes her friends do not share and that bothers her. I reminded Joe that cheaters do not always know better and we need to forgive them. (Obviously a subject for a future homily). I told Sarah that friends who are hurting inside, can mistakenly hurt others without intending to do so. One way to fix that is to ask them how they are and let them talk about the hurt they feel. Suppose Joe that you were extra kind to the cheater, do you think that he might see you as a friend and cheat less when you are together? He was not sure. Sarah, if you were extra kind to your friend who does not share, do you think that she will eventually share with you too? She did not share my enthusiasm, but I suspect that this discussion will turn into a future family discussion. We had a wonderful visit and I enjoyed myself.

Thank you, Father in heaven for another wonderful day. Please care for my Protestant and non-Catholic colleagues, their families and keep them safe. Please care for the families of the parish, especially Bill, Liz, Joe and Sarah, my family and particularly those families who struggle and who do not feel loved.

CHAPTER 33

Preached Love in the family (Saturday/Sunday, September 15-16)

D ear Friends, I read recently that families especially marital relationships are schools of love; families are where we first learn what love is and how to love. Starting with a new born infant, they are totally helpless and absolutely dependent on their parents for survival, nourishment and love. As they grow, they learn new dimensions of love by sharing their toys and interacting with children their own age. They have also been loved by their parents and seen how their parents love one another and the other members of the family. Loving our parents means that we do not want to hurt them or offend them. The family can help us to understand the challenges and the complexities of loving others. Its support and understanding is important when we make mistakes or feeling offended.

What are the benefits of loving others? We learn how to put the needs of others before our own needs, known as maturity. We learn how to live and work comfortably with others. Society works so much better under these conditions. Loving others broadens us; we learn to love others in different cultures and different racial groups. These are all part of the Christian mandate to "love another" or put their needs above your own.

Another benefit of loving others is its healing and accommodating qualities. Being loved means that we change our behavior to reciprocate with that loving person. We learn how to live and accommodate with different living habits. Being loved can heal old hurts and gives us the courage to try loving others again.

This school of love includes learning to forgive, to be tolerant and to be non-judgmental, also very important Christian practices.

CHAPTER 34

Sunday dinner with family
(Sunday, September 16)

Home for dinner with my family. My sister, the perennial tease, asked me what kind of trouble was I in now. I told the family about my meetings and how responsive the members of both the CWL and the Men's club to my question of what do men and women want from marriage. I walked them through the answers. There was a prolonged silence and I was unsure if the silence indicated shock and disappointment or what a great idea. Then Sis spoke, (I can always count on her to speak for the family), you are in trouble, aren't you? Where did you get that idea from? What will the Bishop say about this, she went on, implying I was not to be trusted on my own. My brother, a quieter and more reflective type, piped up saying that we live in a very stuffy church and I suspect that your fresh ideas are giving a new vitality to the practice of our faith in your parish. Thank you Bro. Exactly what I was hoping the Bishop would say too. I asked my parents if they had anything to contribute. Dad said that while he has never heard a sermon or a priest talk about marriage like this but felt that openness and being candid always paid off in the end. Mother, in her typical corrective tone, said, "Son, your father and I will always love you regardless of how much trouble you are in". Thank you, Mother, but I am not in trouble. The men in this family are optimists and the women are pessimists. Is there a lesson here for me? Is my sister trying to help me not become uppity and privileged?

Thank you, Father, in heaven for my parents, my brother and sister, their spouses and my grandchildren.

CHAPTER 35

Day off, meeting with Maggie (Monday, September 17)

I studied for my online scripture course in the morning at my parent's home. The subject this week was Abraham. I lunched with Mother but sensed that the conversation over dinner the night before still disturbed her more than she let on. She never broached the subject other than to ask if the Bishop called. That was enough to tell me that she was worried about me.

At 1:00 pm, I had a phone call from Maggie, a young seventeen-year-old woman from my former parish. She is the daughter of a prominent Catholic family in the city. She said that she has a big problem and could she come by this afternoon? She is a straight A student and class valedictorian. What kind of problems could she be having? I told her to meet me at Fr. Mike's Rectory at 2:00 pm. As scheduled, she knocked on our door and looked distressed as I let her in and directed her to my former office. As soon as we sat down, she began to cry. When she was finally able to catch her breath, she said that she thought that she was pregnant and was scared to death. When her sobbing subsided, she continued. She was at a late-night party with her classmates and some friends. Someone had some crack cocaine and everyone was trying it. I do not remember passing out. When I came to a few hours later, my underwear was missing and my vagina area was sore and wet. It was yucky. When I asked my girlfriends about it, they do not remember very much either. I have missed my last two periods. I am worried sick. No one knows about this especially my parents and my brothers. She said that I was the first person she has talked to and continued to cry. What am I going to do if I am pregnant, she said? I expressed my sorrow for her predicament. My parents, she continued, speak very highly of you and I could not think of one person to whom I could tell my dirty secret. I wonder if it would be better for me to jump off a bridge? I started to get anxious and worried. Maggie, I said, we need some time to think this through. Are you sure that you are pregnant? Have you been to a doctor yet? No, she said, I have been afraid to approach him because he may feel obliged to tell my parents before I am ready. I told her that I knew a number of female gynecologists who would see her without any obligation to tell her parents. We debated that establishing if she was, in fact, pregnant was the first step. After what seemed like forever, she agreed. Cautiously she said, is my dirty little secret safe with you? Yes, of course. Assuredly, I told her that I would treat our conversation like I would a confession. In the meantime, I told her to pray and ask God our loving Father for guidance. Try going to daily Mass and communion. Let God take over. Are you working for City Recreation again this summer? No, only part-time at a day care centre. As she got up to leave, I gave her a big hug. She gave me a tiny smile from a very frightened looking face.

I later had dinner with Fr. Mike at the parish, discussing church humor, church gossip and what's new and exciting in the Vatican, all clerical stuff. It was good to be back with him. He wanted to know about my work in the parish. He said that I sounded quite busy. I talked to him about my online scripture course which he found intriguing. He is a history buff, particularly interested in medieval history and the Renaissance. Before I left, Fr. Mike said that he wanted to give me a head's up. He went on, a gentleman named Jerome approached him last week asking if he would allow having a LGBTQ Catholic support group in the parish and a special mass for them on occasion? He went on to say that his group of about 15 members did not feel welcome in mainstream city parishes. They would be happy to rent a meeting space in the parish. I told him that I would need some time to assess his request. Fr. Mike said to me that he was sorry, but he phoned Jerome back and gave him my telephone number. He is going to phone you tomorrow. This is not a justification for avoiding this matter, but said that he is too old and unwell to manage this type of church stress. He has not approached the Bishop either. I was back home in the parish by 9:00 pm and time to check out the baseball scores, hear about the NFL rumor mill on the sports channel and much needed quiet time with God the Father.

My kind and compassionate Father, please assist me in addressing Maggie's and Jerome's complex problems. As usual, thank you for all the good things that happened today, not the least were my mother, Maggie, Jerome and Fr. Mike. Obviously, Father, my pastoral boundaries are about to be broadened. Please give me the wisdom to be kind and helpful in your service.

CHAPTER 36

Bible study class: Abraham (Tuesday, September 18)

Summary of class notes

The story of Abraham and Sarah is found in the Book of Genesis, chapters 12 to 25, verses 1-11. God started the second phase of his plan for mankind with Abram (soon to be renamed Abraham). God asked him to leave his home in far off Haran in what is thought today to be Armenia and go to a place in Canaan, in what is known today as Lebanon, Jordan and Israel. God assured him of his blessings and of his protection.

Ultimately, he was to become a father of a great nation. His wife Sarai (soon to become Sarah) unfortunately, was barren and they did not have any children. Sarai also believed rightly or wrongly, that God did not want her to have children. Abram, without questioning, packed up his wife, servants, animals and possessions along with his nephew Lot with his wife, servants, animals and possessions and they journeyed together to Canaan. After arriving in Canaan, they discovered it to be in the middle of a famine and they had to move on to Egypt where there was plenty. As Sarai was very beautiful, Abram was suspicious that the Pharaoh would kill him to have Sarai in his harem. To save his life, Abram let it be known to the Pharaoh that Sarai was only his sister. The Pharaoh then took Sarai into his harem and rewarded Abram with sheep, oxen, camels and donkeys as well as man servants and maid servants. But God afflicted the Pharaoh with plagues because of Sarai. Pharaoh found out about Abram's lie, criticized Abram for his deception and kicked him out of Egypt. Abram presented Sarai as his sister a second time with King Abimelech again to save his life. Back in Canaan, Abram and Lot decided to separate grazing lands; Lot chose the plains of Jordan near Sodom and Gomorrah and Abram near Hebron. God made a covenant with Abram promising descendants and land. Sarai grew more frustrated at not bearing an heir for Abram, asked him to marry her Egyptian slave girl, Hagar. When Hagar realized that she was pregnant, she looked with contempt on Sarai because of her barrenness. Hagar soon gave birth to a son, Ishmael. Abram was 86 years old. Eventually Sarai got pregnant and bore a son Isaac. Abram was now 100 years old when Isaac was born. Soon Sarai dismisses Hagar and Ismael. They ran away into the wilderness. An angel of the Lord found them and encouraged Hagar to return to her mistress. God renewed his covenant with Abram, changed his name to Abraham and Sarai's to Sarah. Circumcision was to be the sign of the covenant. Then God and two angels visited Abraham who welcomed them graciously. They mentioned that they are on their way to check out Sodom and Gomorrah. They have heard dreadful things and were prepared to destroy it. Abraham fearing for the lives of Lot and his family, started negotiations with God requesting that the cities be saved if there are 50 good people living there? Yes, replied God. What about 45? Yes, God agreed to 45. What about 40? Yes, 40. Eventually, Abraham skillfully negotiated God down to 10 people. But in the end, the cities were destroyed. Sarah sent Hagar and Ishmael away again. Again, the angel of God found them, saved them and promised that Ishmael would be a father of a great nation. God then to test Abraham, asked him to sacrifice the life of his son Isaac. Human sacrifice was a common practice at the time. Abraham agreed but, in the end, God provided a ram for the sacrifice.

My takeaways:

1. Abraham listened to God and had a relationship with him with the result that God protected him. God wants a relationship us too and will protect us too;
2. God seemed to accommodate his mistakes when he lied to protect his life from the Pharaoh and King Abimelech and seemed very understanding to his failures. God can do the same with our mistakes and our obstacles; and
3. Abraham was so comfortable with his relationship with God that he was able to negotiate with God about saving Sodom and Gomorrah. Why can't we negotiate with God for the benefit of others?

CHAPTER 37

Pastoral Council meeting (Wednesday, September 18)

Jerome phoned me early this morning and requested an appointment with me. Could he come tomorrow morning? I said yes and we scheduled to meet at 10:00 am tomorrow, Thursday.

Well, we had a very interesting parish council meeting: After an introduction to many of the men's group members, a short prayer led by Fred, parish finances were first up on the agenda. Fred asked the treasurer Stan Hart to present their recommended monthly financial plan: The parish wants to provide the accommodation for the parish priest (estimated cost: $200.00 mobile home lease), bank loan ($250.00), utilities including heat, telephone, TV and electricity ($300.00), the Bishop's administration fee ($300.00) and church maintenance ($200.00) for a total of $1,250.00 a month. The parish will pay me $2,950.00 a month to pay food ($1,200.00), car ($250.00 bank loan), gas ($100.00), car insurance ($100.00) and pension ($300.00). Total monthly expenses $1,950.00. Fred inquired if $1,950.00 would be sufficient? I was shocked and blurted out that I thought so. Fred indicated that the collections from both parishes equals about $3,500.00 a month, meaning that the families are not subsidizing the parish to meet its monthly obligations. The Christmas and Easter collections normally bring in an additional 15% more thereby allowing the parish to save for future maintenance expenses to the church. Fred asked for my thoughts and I thanked them for their generosity and said that if finances became a problem, I could plant a vegetable garden instead of growing grass. They had a good chuckle. I gave them an official overview of activities of the CWL, the men's club as well the inter-denominational group. They seemed pleased. I asked them for comments about the last bulletin and women's and men's marital needs. Big silence. Fred broke the uncomfortable silence by saying that my ideas were quite foreign to this rural parish. Father, you need to bring us up to speed on your plans for the parish and your vision of a parish community. We are not opposed to what you are advocating; we are just not on your page yet. We need more time and more discussion. I agreed and apologized if I have been too pushy and insensitive. Would you agree, I continued, if we postponed a discussion on the health and stability of marriages in the parish and in the community. Yes, please. But he also asked that our marriage suggestions not be published in our local newspaper. I agreed. I then alerted the Council to a desire of our inter-denominational group to have an appreciation night to honor the people who work on behalf of the community, such as hospital staff, the school staff, the RCMP, the editor of the local newspaper, Town staff and Town Council and to thank them for their service to the community. They unanimously thought it was a great idea and offered to help. I also alerted them to the difficult financial situation of the Anglican church. I explained what Claire reported to me, namely that their numbers are too small to support her and the church. I also offered our church for their use provided you the Parish Council and the Bishop agreed. Fred said that they would need to agree to pay their share of utilities, cleaning and other expenses. I asked for a vote and a majority voted yes provided there were no problems with it. Fred and Stan agreed to talk to Claire. I asked them to wait until the Bishop had endorsed it too. I concluded by stating that I would raise this issue with the Bishop at my next opportunity.

Thank you, Father, in heaven for the kind and concerned parish volunteers on the Pastoral Council. What are we humans that you care for us so much? You have made us into you image and likeness and crowned us with glory and honor. You have given us dominion over all creatures and the works of your hands. We praise your name over all the earth.

CHAPTER 38

Meeting with Jerome (Wednesday, September 19)

Today I had planned to devote my attention to my online scripture course. The class schedule was to study of Abraham and his role in God's plan for the salvation of humankind. At 10:00 am, Jerome and Raymond knocked on my door. They explained over tea the discomfort they have felt at many parishes in the city. They are not greeted as they enter the church like others are. They are not invited to become active in the life of the parishes and requests for a meeting with the pastor are ignored. So, would I consider allowing the LGBTQ community to meet here and having an occasional mass for them in your parish? I apologized for the way the Church has treated them. It is bigotry at its worst and contrary to the core teachings of the Church that teaches love and acceptance. I assured them that God our father loved them exactly like they are. They continued that they would like to feel welcome in a Catholic Church as many of them were raised Catholic. They also wanted to receive the sacraments and be supportive of the broader LGBTQ community in the city. After hearing their full story, I told them that we have basically two choices: first, my preference is to approach the Bishop and get his permission or agreement given the negative Catholic teaching on homosexuality or, second, I invite you and your group to come here on a bi-weekly basis where we can operate quietly and under the radar, so to speak. I explained that I prefer to be open and transparent about what I do but I have come to realize that it is not always possible to do so. I explained to them that the Bishop is very reasonable and open-minded and has never forbidden me from doing anything that was helpful and had a good pastoral basis. After a back and forth debate, they acceded to my preference. I asked them to provide me with their contact information and to give a week to ten days to find an answer. We agreed to meet next time in the city at a convenient location. They thanked me for my time. I thanked them for their grit and determination in seeking me out. After they had left, I phoned Fr. Mike. As soon as he heard my voice, he apologized again. Can you please, I asked, make yourself available for a meeting next week with the Bishop? He agreed. I phoned Margaret and asked for 45 minutes for a meeting with the Bishop, Fr. Mike and myself, preferably on next Monday. I thanked her for giving us his 4:00 pm time slot. Fr. Mike was available too and I arranged to drive him to this meeting.

Thank you, Father, in heaven for making our lives so much easier.

CHAPTER 39

Deanery meeting and Homily prep with Fred's family (Thursday September 20)

Our first Deanery meeting began at noon. Present were Bishop Ben, Fathers George West (St. Mary's Parish), Mark de Santos (Holy Family Parish), Raj Patel (St Thomas

Parish) and me. The Bishop provided deli meat sandwiches while I provided some of Mother's minestrone soup and beer from a local small brewery. Everyone was in a relaxed mood. The Bishop lead off by saying that the finances in the diocese were currently in good shape. He is still however, dealing with some legal and financial consequences from the behaviors of some former predatory priests. He thinks that the spiritual and financial well-being of the diocese is due to strong relationships with the laity. The Diocesan Pastoral Council, he continued, has warned him that while the finances are fine now, the long term look bleak and our current financial numbers will decline. Why? We have an aging population and fewer young singles and married people in the church. While we have many immigrant Canadians joining our parishes, they send their surplus monies home to their families in their respective countries of origin. The closure of parishes is looming as the mean age of our priests is now sixty-two and we are getting fewer candidates for the priesthood from Canada. We cannot always rely on India, Africa, South America and the Philippines to supplement our declining numbers of priests. So, he suggested that we try to make our respective churches a more attractive spiritual home. He also encouraged us work on seeking the advice of successful members of their parishes. I asked him if we could survey our current parishioners on how to make our church more attractive? Yes, Fr. Cam, you have my support. He also alerted everyone about our community public service appreciation night being planned in late September by St. Francis. Everyone thought it was a great idea and asked to hear about its success at our next Deanery meeting in October. Another item of importance, the Bishop continued, is the use of the internet. He would like us to use it more. Please communicate with him by emails whenever possible. Use a word document for your monthly reports. This will improve our communications. However, we will still meet regularly face to face and of course use the telephone. He concluded his comments by saying that he would be in Ontario for a Bishop's meeting in early October. He then asked what we needed to carry our parish duties? Fr George talked about needing more computer training. Fr. Raj said that he needed coaching in English as it is neither his first nor his second language. I suggested that a course in active listening and dealing with family problems would be helpful too. We decided that a presentation on the role of the priest in family disputes by a psychologist or therapist would be the subject of our October agenda. Fr. George agreed to host it.

This evening I visited Fred and Hilary's home where I met their two sons, Chad and Chuck. I thanked them for their time as the five of us sat around a table in their large kitchen. I explained the nature of my visit was to ask their help in preparing my sermon. With their help, I would be able express the Christian message on Sunday in a manner that the parish would understand and get excited about. I shared my suspicion that Christ's message has been masked with old rules and practices that do not resonate with people today. I told them that my theme was service and the Gospel reading was about Christ washing the feet of the apostles. Hilary read the text and then silence. It seemed that they were all waiting for the other to speak first. Both Fred and Hillary agreed that the core message needed repackaging. How, I replied? I looked to Chad and Chuck. They looked at one another and then Chuck the older began. He agreed that the message was obscure and has not been well presented. As a 21-year-old, I am trying to figure out what life is all about and how I will live my life. For me, the church is not a source of inspiration or advice. It is too hung up on sex. Sex is bad. Don't have sex. Do not use condoms. He took a breath and smiled at himself, as if surprised by what he had said. OK Chuck, I replied, what do you suggest? I think the Church should operate like a grocery store or a hospital. You go there when you need to but there should be no obligation to do so. One should not be looked down upon if they do not attend Sunday mass every Sunday. The beliefs and truth should be laid out so that when I need them, I can find them easily. I think my parents are good Catholics and have given my brother and I wonderful opportunities for which I am truly grateful and will be all my life. Chad spoke next. He agreed with his brother and said priests should be more visible and more approachable, like goodwill ambassadors. I think if they were married like you and had a wife and children, they would understand what the average people are going through in life. Chad, I corrected, I had a wife until she died but I do not and did not have children. Whatever, he continued, you seem more approachable than previous priests. Then there is no divorce allowed in the Church. How are we at our age to know who is suitable to spend the rest of our lives with. What if she turns into someone horrible? I think the no divorce rule is not practical, like no-trade clauses in pro sports. Finally, I jumped in; Why can't you guys live your beliefs? No one is going to stand at the door and ask you the last time you came to church. I will not judge you if I see you only occasionally at Mass. Live our faith the best you can. The visit continued by discussing the challenges of farming and ranching when the business world is changing so fast. As I left, I thanked them for their time and their thoughtful ideas and suggestions. I hoped we could continue this discussion again soon. I reminded them that these types of frank discussions help me to be a better priest. As I write this journal entry, I was not sure if this evening, as pleasant as it was, has helped me to prepare Sunday's homily, but it was really good for me professionally and pastorally.

Father in heaven, thank you for Fred, Hilary, Chuck and Chad. Please keep watch over them. Cam

CHAPTER 40

Free day, study and laundry
(Friday, September 21)

A Friday with nothing scheduled for a change. Time for some laundry and meal planning for next week.

Father in heaven, am I moving too fast in promoting what appears to me to be my particular agenda, my brand of love? Please give me some cues. So, we are back to the core message of love; loving our Father in heaven and loving/serving our neighbor. Why did I not mention that relationships are a school of love to Chuck and Chad?

CHAPTER 41

Preached "God of surprises"
(Saturday/Sunday, September 22/23)

D ear Friends, as some of you know, I am studying the Old Testament by correspondence. So far, we have studied Adam and Eve, Noah, Abraham, Jacob, Joseph and eventually Moses. An overview of the intra-family dynamics has interesting lessons. I would like to use this opportunity to share with you what I have learned. My key takeaway is that our loving God is a God of surprises.

These stories are fiction. There is no scientific evidence to them. We believe however that God has inspired these stories with religious truths.

The book of Genesis begins with two stories of creation; one explains the basic creation of the world from nothing by an all-powerful God and the second presents a God who after he had created animals and plants, decided something was missing, so he created Adam. But he realized that he still had not done enough and so he created Eve and used one of Adam's rib to create her to show the intimate connection and relationship between men and women. He put them in the Garden of Eden that had everything they needed. God also wanted a relationship with them. You will remember that they were instructed not to eat the fruit of the tree of good and evil. Why they rebelled and disobeyed is not explained but it changed God's relationship with them. Life was going to be more difficult. In spite of that, God helps them to cover their nakedness. As all actions both good and bad have consequences, good and bad karma, relationships with God became more complicated.

In the story of Noah, God explains that he is unhappy with the way mankind is treating one another. Too much evil, so he wants to wipe out civilization and start over. Noah is obedient; he is known as walking with God. God orders him to build an Ark, which he does. He loads his extended family and representatives of all the animals into the Ark and then a 40-day flood occurs. God guides Noah as they rebuild the earth and life on it. Interestingly, God seemingly regrets using the flood to wipe out life as it was known. He promises never to do that again, makes a covenant with Noah and uses a rainbow to signify it.

The story of Abraham is fascinating. He is chosen to be the father of the Jewish people in spite of having a wife called Sarai that is barren. She is scorned because of this barrenness. God asks Abram as he is known as the story begins (think Abe Lincoln) to leave his home in what is known today as Armenia and move his family, his servants and animals to Canaan in what today is known as Israel. He takes his nephew Lot with him. Due to a famine in Canaan, they move to Egypt.

Abram fears for his life because he thinks that the Pharaoh will kill him to have Sarai as part of his haram as she is drop-dead gorgeous. Abram lies to spare his life and spreads the message that Sarai is only his sister. As expected, the Pharaoh takes Sarai into his harem. God watching over this situation sends plagues on the Pharaoh and his family. The Pharaoh kicks Abraham out of Egypt. Sarai is desperate to have a child and in desperation, she asks Abram to marry her slave Hagar who becomes pregnant and now looks with contempt on Sarai. Sarai becomes Sarah and eventually conceives Isaac when she is ninety years and Abraham is one hundred years old. Imagine having a son at that age. Nothing is impossible with God. God seems to ignore the evil behavior of both Abraham and Sarah.

Next generation: Isaac and Rebekah have twin boys, Esau and Jacob. Isaac favors Esau the outdoors type whereas Rebekah favors Jacob. Esau in a moment of weakness sells his birthright to Jacob (his rights as first-born son) and Rebekah deceitfully assists Jacob to steal Esau's patriarchal blessing. This blessing from a father's death bed invokes fertility of the land, the ruling over other nations and finally God's blessing and protection. God accommodates these family shenanigans.

Jacob escapes the wrath of Esau and goes to Haran where Rebekah's brother Laban lives. He meets Rachel his daughter, is smitten and agrees to work seven years for her hand in marriage. In the darkness of the wedding night, Laban substitutes his eldest daughter, Leah. So, Jacob agrees to work another seven years for the hand of Rachel. There is more intrigue and deviousness occurring between the herds of Laban and Jacob until Jacob returns to Canaan. Unfortunately, family life is not easy: he has two wives (as challenge in itself), one who is very fruitful and the other barren. Leah has eleven boys (girls are not counted) that become the eleven tribes of Israel. Rachel is barren but eventually gets pregnant and gives birth to Joseph. Internal family strife continues; Jacob favors Joseph (not a good thing). Joseph dreams of greatness that antagonizes his brothers resulting in their selling of him to a caravan of Ishmaelites transporting goods to Egypt. The brothers report that Joseph was killed by a wild animal.

Joseph is purchased by an Egyptian in the Pharaoh's household and ultimately becomes very successful in Egypt because God is watching over him. During a famine in Canaan, Jacob sends two of his sons to Egypt to buy food. Joseph recognizes them and the family is re-united. Many generations later, the Jewish people are taken advantage of by the Pharaoh at the time, God then calls Moses.

What are the lessons to be learned here?

1. Sarah and Rachel suffered the experience of barrenness in a society where having children was a necessity. Barren-ness made one an outcaste in the culture of the Israelites. God eventually rewarded them with children in spite of their intrigue and bad behavior. They, sadly, were not able to see beyond the barren-ness to the plan that God had for them.
2. Isaac, Rebekah, Jacob and Rachel played favorites among their children, causing no end to family strife.
3. God in spite of these behaviors, remained true to his covenant with Noah, never to destroy mankind, no matter how bad things got.
4. God watched over, protected, blessed and worked with this extended family, despite its many mistakes.
5. Do not despair when family relationships go sideways; they need time.

CHAPTER 42

Day off; study; visit family; meeting with the Bishop and Fr. Mike; dinner with Fr. Mike's (Monday, September 24)

Nothing like a good family visit to calm my nerves, sleep in my old bed, still studying Abraham and his negotiations with God. Very enlightening.

At 2:00 pm, Maggie came back for another visit. She looked calmer and in a better space. She had been to a gynecologist and yes, the Doctor confirmed that she was pregnant. I told her how sorry I was. She calmly said that she was too young to have a baby and become a mother. Besides, she did not know who the father was. This will kill my parents. She continued, this is not what my parents had planned for their eldest child and their only girl. I knew her parents, Paul and Simone and yes, they would be devastated. After what seemed like a painful pause, she continued. Two of my friends have advised me to have an abortion. The church is opposed to abortion, right? Yes, I said. All life is sacred whether it is human life, animal life or plant life. After another pause, I could tell she was carefully choosing her words. Are there any exceptions to this rule? You know my dad, a practicing lawyer, says there are always exceptions to every rule or situation in life. She was right; Paul made a successful career out of cleaning up legal messes. He found ways to fix and repair difficult situations that most good lawyers would not touch. She paused and said that she has been at the public library studying the subject of abortion and then asked, when does life begin? I said at conception and according to the Church's teaching, you now have a tiny human person with a soul in your tummy. There are however, highly respected Catholic theologians who study the Church's teachings and argue that human life begins only after three months. Since there is no way to determine definitively when life begins, the Church has taken the safest position that life begins at conception. I asked her if she had plans to study in the Fall. Yes, she said. She has been accepted into a pre-law program at McGill University in Montreal. Did she know anyone in Montreal that she could live with who would protect her privacy? She did not. Do you parents know anything yet? No. Have you had morning sickness? No, she said, only slightly. She has been very fortunate. She continued, can I be a good Catholic and believe in abortion? I said yes, there are teachings that even I disagree with. She said, like what? The teachings on sexuality. I believe that they are 200 years out of date. Is anything that's helping you manage this troubling situation on a daily basis? Is your prayer life helping? Yes, thank you for encouraging that. Our visit ended. Another quick hug and she was gone.

The Bishop seemed very relaxed as we were ushered into his office. Max was there to greet us and demand a nuzzle from us until he received his customary ear rub. In response to the Bishop's question, what's up, I outlined the story of Jerome and Raymond. He listened intently as he normally does. I rambled on; the Vatican's attitude and approach to LGBTQ people in my opinion is contrary to the basic Christian message, namely that God created us all equal, loves as we are and who are we to judge what goes on in people's personal lives. St John's Epistles are significant too; where there is love (in relationships), God is present, because God is love. The Gospels are filled with stories of Jesus caring for outsiders of his time, namely lepers, the disabled and foreigners such as the Canaanite woman. This is equally as scandalous as the sexual abuse of minors. I quoted Pope John XXIII who protected Jewish refugees fleeing from Nazi persecution during World War II by giving them false baptismal certificates. This saintly Pope had a dictum, "See everything, overlook a great deal and correct a little." I stopped to catch my breath allowing Bishop Ben to ask what I suggesting. Please allow me, I continued, to provide the sacraments, spiritual support and the occasional mass for this group of outsiders. Social justice demands that we provide our spiritual services to them. We will operate quietly, but I will have to alert the leaders of the parish to what is going on. Bishop Ben turned to Fr. Mike and asked him what he thought of these suggestions. Fr. Mike said that is a very difficult situation. He did not know what was worse: ignoring this important pastoral need or ignoring the Church's teaching, raising his hands as if to imply a struggle going on in his mind. We are a religious community that welcomes newcomers into our midst; that is how we spread the Gospel; that is our mandate. If any priest of the diocese were to tackle this matter, I cannot think of a better person, a better priest than Cam to do it. The Bishop put his hand up stopping the conversation. I am thinking of damage control, he said. What is the worst thing that can happen here? Fr. Mike responded, that the press gets wind of this and describes St. Francis Parish as a gay parish and worse yet that Fr. Cam is a gay priest. The bishop got up and started to pace. Then he abruptly closed the meeting. Thank you both for coming in today on your day off. I will phone you both Wednesday with my decision and instructions. Thank you for your courage and strength. I admire you both very much. We were abruptly ushered out the door. My dinner with Fr. Mike was strangely quiet. We were both taken aback by his sudden closure of our meeting. So, we determined that this needed to be a two-cocktail dinner.

Driving back to the parish I wondered what the Bishop was now thinking. I arrived back at the rectory to see Ed Malone waiting for me. Good news, he said. The national newspaper based in Toronto, the Tribune, would like to do a feature story on me for a weekend edition. Are you up to it? I just looked at him in shock. Ed, the article will have to be about Bishop

Ben and me. Please phone him tomorrow, no next week and discuss it with him.

Father in heaven, please guide me through these complex situations. The Bishop sticks his neck out for me a lot and I am wondering if he is having some regrets about inviting me into his diocese. Please take care of Bishop Ben, Fr. Mike, Jerome and his community and of course my friend, Ed. Thank you for listening. Amen.

CHAPTER 43

Scripture class "Moses" (Tuesday, Sept. 25)

The Bishop phoned me at 9:00 am saying that he had just talked to Fr. Mike and they had agreed that the Bishop appoint me the official diocesan representative for this group. The group should come up with a special name for themselves. They could have their meetings in the parish and have occasional special masses. Parties of the group however, should be held a facility in the city. Fr. Cam, are you in agreement? Yes, Bishop, I am. Thank you. I will phone Jerome and pass on the message and get back to you with the name that they chose. I phoned Jerome and told him the good news. I asked him to phone me with the official name of their group so that I, in turn, could pass it on to the Bishop.

The Bishop also asked me to phone Ed to request a postponement of the joint interview for the Toronto Tribune.

Scripture Class subject: "Moses"

Summary of class notes:

The story pf Moses is found in the Book of Exodus, chapters 1-24 and chapters 31-34 and the Book of Deuteronomy. Between Abraham and Moses, God's plan for mankind continues; Joseph, according to God's plan, ends up in Egypt ultimately becoming Pharaoh's right-hand man. When Canaan was affected with a famine, Jacob sent some of his sons to Egypt for food. Joseph soon forgives his brothers and the family moves to Egypt. As years go by, the Hebrews become a very large population. A new Pharaoh is worried about an ever-growing population of Israelites and to get control of them, imposes onerous work conditions on them and ultimately orders the Hebrew midwives to kill all Hebrew male children.

The story of Moses takes place between 1552 and 1304 BCE. There is no archeological evidence of the exodus of the Israelites from Egypt. The Israelites had been in Egypt for approximately 400 years up to the time of Moses

A Hebrew woman has a male child and in order to protect him from death, puts him in a waterproof basket and leaves him on the Nile River where the Pharaoh's daughter normally bathes. The woman's daughter quietly watches over him. The Pharaoh's daughter discovers him and asks the young girl to find a woman to nurse the child. Soon, the child joins the Pharaoh's family and is named Moses. As an adult, he notices one day an Egyptian fighting a Hebrew and kills the Egyptian. He is now being hunted by the Pharaoh. The Hebrews do not trust him either because of his connection to the Pharaoh. He escapes to an area known as the Midian where he is taken in by a family. While working as a shepherd, God appeared to him in a burning bush, explaining that he had heard his Israelite people in Egypt call out for help. He asked Moses to approach the Pharaoh, getting his permission to depart for three days of prayer to their God in the wilderness on Mount Horeb. The Pharaoh refuses due to work commitments and even makes their lives more difficult by disallowing straw to be used in the making of bricks. God then introduces 10 plagues on the Egyptian people to change Pharaoh's mind. The 10th plague was the killing of all firstborn children including the Pharaoh's, that resulted in his release of the Israelite people. However, after they had departed, the Pharaoh changed his mind and he set out with his armies to capture the fleeing Israelites. The Pharaoh's army is destroyed at the Red Sea by God's direct intervention. Moses led them to Mount Sinai where the Israelites renewed their covenant with God. While Moses was on the mountain praying to God for 40 days and 40 nights, the Israelites failed to trust God and fell back into their old spiritual practices and with Aaron's help, built a calf out of gold. God was furious with them. Moses went to bat for them and was able to convince God to forgive and try again to renew the covenant. God is presented as gracious, merciful, faithful and forgiving. God gives them again the 10 commandments as a means of maintaining one's relationship with God and one's neighbor. This practice would lead to happiness, the opposite of slavery in Egypt. God also reveals his name as Yahweh (The ancients believed that to know the name of the deity, enabled one to influence the deity). The Israelites spend 40 years in the desert, fed by God with water from a rock, manna in the morning and quail in the evening. Moses led them to the edge of Canaan.

Takeaways: On Mount Sinai, God presents himself first as this very powerful deity that can operate outside the scope of our experience as he sent these plagues, saved the Israelites at the Red Sea and fed them water from a rock, with manna and quail in the desert. This side of God is reminiscent of early Genesis where God creates the world. On the other hand, God is also presented as our friend and life's companion, willing to understand, forgive our mistakes, even changes his mind and accommodates our fear of commitment to him.

CHAPTER 44

Prepare report to Bishop
re September activities
(Wednesday, September 26)

I began to prepare for my next meeting with the Bishop where I would review my September parish activities: a public service appreciation night, parish finances, CWL and Susan, Fred's speaking out about my teachings on living married love, an update on my presentation on married love at the next Deanery meeting, and the Good Samaritan Group.

I phoned Ed Malone and relayed the Bishop's request to postpone the joint interview. He asked if there was an appeal process? No, there is not. The Bishop is the person we appeal to for a second opinion. Ed asked if a Cardinal was higher in the chain of command than a Bishop and how Bishop Ben would react if he were to appeal to his friend the Cardinal in Toronto? He went on the explain that when the Cardinal was appointed to Toronto some years ago, he interviewed him for the Toronto Tribune. They became good friends and still are. The Cardinal still sends him a Christmas card every year. I encouraged him to talk to his friend the Cardinal about his proposed feature article.

Father in heaven, thank you for Bishop Ben, the CWL, Susan, Nurse Rita, Fred, the Good Samaritan Group and Ed.

CHAPTER 45

Homily prep, Mabel's home (Thursday, September 27)

At 7:00 pm. I was welcomed into Mabel's and Ned's spacious home. As we sat down with tea, Ned introduced himself; he is an agronomist and travels for a large international seed and fertilizer company. They have two married daughters who have five grandchildren that Mabel and Ned do not see enough of. Their girls and their families live four hours away. Their spacious home allows them to host the two other families both in the summer and at Christmas time. While they miss their grandchildren, they love this close-knit community and expect to retire here. This evening Mabel looked less like a stern "Mother Superior" than before.

Given that our theme for this upcoming Sunday is love in the family, would you like to share with me the success of your marriage? They seemed uncertain and at a loss for words, so I inquired if they would introduce their marriage to me. Ned began by saying that they were married quite young and will be celebrating our 35th wedding anniversary next year. Mabel added that the marriage has not always been a smooth ride as Ned travels a lot. I was expected to be both mother and father to the girls. To be fair, he was home most weekends, but his presence seemed to upset our daily rituals and routines. It was stressful. Ned admitted that he felt like an outsider during those years. The three girls got along really well and I sometimes felt like a disturber. I think in retrospect, that it was more my feelings than anything said by them. On the other hand, being away as much as I was, I was relieved that they were like three peas in a pod. Mabel went on to explain that what Ned was describing was a particular stage in their marriage. We always had wonderful summer vacations with the girls. They frequently each brought a friend. Ned would take a month off work which helped us to reconnect. Ned was very patient with us and seemed to know when to leave our routines alone. Our faith was a big help. We both were raised in staunch Catholic homes where there was daily prayer particularly at bedtime. Growing up, bedtime prayers were a combination of prayers and a chat about what we and our friends did both at school and after school. I used to joke with Ned that the girls learned about public confession long after the practice stopped. Looking back, in my opinion, more talking and more discussion would have eased the stress. Ned added that more time away from the girls may have helped us. Mabel and I have always had something very special together even going back to our dating days. We were always very compatible. Mabel continued that while Ned's profession took him away from us a lot, it provided us with a very comfortable life style. Would we have been just as happy with less money and him at home all the time? Possibly. Possibly not. What is the expression, "Hindsight is 20-20"? I think a successful marriage is one where the partners learn to live with the abilities and the constraints of each partner as well as accommodating their changes as we age. I then inquired if they thought a couple's weekend retreat would be something we should promote in the parish? They agreed and Mabel suggested that the CWL could organize it? Would the attendees give the talks? They agreed and suggested opening the weekend to other couples in the community. I agreed and could I invite the Bishop for this weekend if he is free from other responsibilities? Of course, they responded.

Father in heaven, you are truly a God of surprises. I returned to the rectory feeling elated again. Mabel and Ned have such invigorating energy. I loved spending this time with them. Thank you, Father, for another day working with you.

CHAPTER 46

Quiet day, study (Friday, September 28)

I made an innocent phone call to Paul and Simone's home to inquire how the family was doing. Simone said that they all were doing well, Paul has had some invigorating contracts, the boys have discovered baseball and Maggie has got into McGill pre-law as a late entry. I have been busy teaching tennis to a group of seniors three mornings a week and holding this ship together. Maggie left last week. Good, one less worry for me. Maggie has all the skills to handle this problem and ultimately will make the right decision for her.

Thank you, Father, for caring for Maggie. Help her make the right decision.

CHAPTER 47

My poor performance homily (Saturday/Sunday, September 29/30)

Father in heaven, I had a very busy week and was completely unprepared to speak for you to the kind and patient parishioners of St. Francis and St. Josephs. I blundered along trying to "wing it" for five minutes, then explained that I was not well prepared due to busyness and poor planning. I concluded by apologizing profusely.

As the parishioners were leaving, many came forward to

assure me that the God loves us and wants to be our companion (my default message). They advised that they cannot hear this message enough.

Father, these parishioners of yours are very tolerant and accommodating. Thank so much.

CHAPTER 48

Day off (Monday, October 01)

After breakfast with mother, I phoned Sis and asked if I could have a quiet dinner with them tonight. She said yes but come at 5:30 to help the children with their homework. I have learned that the pre-dinner period in a busy family can be a crises time with everyone wanting to talk about the good and the bad that happened that day. So, I arrived at 5:00 pm with Carol getting a dinner organized and the children Brad (11 years) and Bonnie (8 years) busy with their homework. I sat down with the kids and began to ask them what they did today at school. They were delighted to have a distraction from their assignments while still under the watchful eye of their mother. Any opportunity to be able to chat instead of study was always welcome. Banker husband was working late and we had a simple pasta dinner with veggies. After an hour of listening to these two little adults, I thanked them for dinner, their time and left. I wanted the two of them to finish their homework or I would be in trouble with their mother.

Jerome phoned me to say that the name chosen for their group was the Good Samaritan Club. I told him that I thought that they had made an excellent choice. I thanked him and emailed the Bishop.

Father, thank you for my parents, my siblings and grandchildren but especially my mother and her enduring kindness and tolerance of her self-destructive son, the priest.

CHAPTER 49

Scripture course subject "Jonah" (Tuesday, October 02)

The story of Jonah is found in the Book of Jonah in the Old Testament. Jonah is considered a minor prophet. This beautiful story is neither history nor geography. This is an example of humorous biblical fiction, that is meant to both entertain and instruct. It was written between 300 and 250 BCE. God calls Jonah to go to Nineveh, the capital of Assyria and to preach to the Ninevites that "their wickedness has become known to me and they need to change their ways". The Assyrians had conquered the Israelites. Without responding, Jonah decides to run away from God. Instead of going east to Nineveh, he goes west. He goes to Joppa where he pays passage on a boat sailing to Tarshish, a place probably either in Spain or in Tunisia. On route, God sends a mighty storm and the sailors do everything in their power to keep the ship afloat. They begin throwing some of their cargo overboard, they pray to their gods and in desperation they throw lots to ascertain where the problem is. The lot falls on Jonah. They suspect that he has done a horrible act to cause his God to send the storm. They begin to pray to Jonah's God too. Jonah confesses that he is running away from his God and suggests that they throw him overboard. They finally agree and throw him overboard but God is still watching over Jonah and sends a large fish to swallow him. The storm subsides and the sailors thank Jonah's God and offer sacrifice. Jonah meantime, spends three days in the belly of this fish before it burps him out on land. God again orders Jonah to go to Nineveh and this time Jonah complies and preaches, "Only 40 days more and Nineveh will be destroyed". Contrary to expectations, the Ninevites believed in God, proclaimed a fast and put on sackcloth, from the greatest to the least. The King also complied and ordered everyone in the land to do penance; even the beasts and flocks were to taste nothing, eat nothing and drink no water. Jonah, in spite of being successful, became depressed. He was expecting that the Ninevites would return to their evil ways and God would destroy Nineveh. But instead, God granted them forgiveness for their penitential ways, making him look foolish. He knew that God was gracious, kind and compassionate.

Takeaways:

1). God is companionable and continues to engage humans in his plan for salvation; this time it is Jonah's turn;
2). In spite of God choosing the Israelite people as his special people, his ultimate plan was for all mankind, including the Assyrians, to benefit from his love, compassion and benevolence. God's love and compassion is not earned but is freely given. This was a difficult pill for the leaders of the Israelites to swallow;
3). Everyone including the captain and sailors on the ship as well as the Ninevites, their animals and flocks respond by praying to God; and
4). God was involved in every stage of Jonah's life as a prophet even when he was running away. God is protective and solicitous even using extraordinary

measures such as a whale to save and protect Jonah.

5). Like Jonah, we need to guard against becoming angry when good things happen to others that we do not think are deserved.

6). Jonah is like us. God calls, we avoid with excuses or get too busy. God persists. God works beyond the boundaries of the Catholic Church.

CHAPTER 50

Monthly meeting with the Bishop (Wednesday, October 03)

After the usual good morning formalities with Margaret, the Bishop's secretary (Would like coffee? Yes, please. Cream and sugar? Just black please). The Bishop began, here we are on another of your days off. No rest for the wicked, that includes me as well if that makes you feel better. Of course, I had to give Max his expected hug and ear rub, before I launched into a review of my September parish activities. I gave him a one sheet summary of the key points. I then outlined the plan for the public service appreciation night, the proposed organization of the parish finances, re-designing the Parish Council to have half men and half women, CWL and Susan, Fred Bartlett's asking me to put the brakes on my teachings on married love, an update on my presentation on married love at the next Deanery meeting. The Bishop listened carefully as was his usual practice. He thought that married love would be a good topic for our next deanery study day in October. I reminded him that we had decided at our first meeting to have a professional therapist to discuss their role as opposed to the role of the priest in resolving marital disputes. Did he want to postpone that subject until November? Yes, please postpone it and let us begin with a presentation of married love. Martial disputes would be a natural follow-up subject. Would I organize and lead a discussion on the subject? Could I bring some married people from the parish, I asked? Yes, if you recommend it and please email me and the other members an agenda for the Deanery meeting and the change of meeting location to St. Francis. Regarding the feature article for the Toronto Tribune, he continued, what are your thoughts? It might sell newspapers but will it help the Church and the Diocese, I replied. He said, let's wait on this a bit. Please contact Mr. Malone and tell him that his suggestion is still under consideration. The Bishop advised me that he would be in Ontario at a Bishop's meeting and he would consult other Bishops on the value of this feature article. He loved the new name for the Good Samaritan Club. Father Cam, he began slowely, I have been thinking about your work with this group. I am going to recommend to all the priests in the diocese that they support special groups in their work.

Thank you, Father in heaven for Bishop Ben and please continue to guide me with your assistance in the pastoral work that we do together.

CHAPTER 51

Office work and CWL meeting (Thursday, October 04)

I prepared an agenda for the next Deanery meeting and emailed it to the Bishop and my fellow priests in the Deanery.

Our agenda: 12:00 to 12:45 lunch and visit (I am barbequing hamburgers both beef and vegetarian along with a salad), 12:45 to 1:30 Church business, 1:30 to 3:00 Married love with the assistance of three married couples from my parish. I emailed Fred and Thelma, Bill and Liz and Ned and Mabel, asking them if they could attend an afternoon from 1:30 to 3:00 of the local area priests and the Bishop. The subject for discussion was to be married love and who better to lead such a discussion but some married couples. Certainly not some celibate men. I will be leading this discussion and I will be asking what the church can do for you to help fulfill your marital and family responsibilities. It would be great if each of you could tell us what works and does not work in developing a loving marriage and family life. The date is October 24 in our parish rectory. If all of you agree, I will send out the agenda. If you would like, I would be happy to organize a short meeting prior to the 24th of the three of you to brainstorm your thoughts and ideas.

The CWL meeting

Mabel had phoned me to advise me that I need not show up for the first hour as they would be addressing national council requests. I joined them at 8:00 pm. We jointly established our agenda: 1. CWL representatives on the Parish Council; 2. Update on current parish activities: the Good Samaritan Club, the Volunteer Appreciation Night, Susan, the upcoming Deanery meeting and its focus on marriage and family life.

They agreed to send three of their members to each meeting but preferred to rotate their representative so that all of them could keep up to date on parish activities. Mabel, Liz and Hilary would attend the next meeting. They seemed surprised that an LGBTQ association was meeting in their boardroom but felt better when they heard that the Bishop had approved it. They responded positively about the Volunteer Appreciation Night and their small part in the food preparation part. Again, hearing from Nurse Ruth that Susan was doing well cheered them. They had little to say about the Deanery meeting.

Father in heaven, I sense the CWL's suspicion of me when we first got together. Give me patience and help me to avoid dwelling on the negativity here. On a positive note, they seem to be warming up to me. Thank you, Father.

CHAPTER 52

Article Prairie News, Good Samaritan Club meeting (Friday, October 05)

Ed Malone put a very nice short article in his weekly newspaper about the upcoming Volunteer Appreciation Night. He listed all the people who would be feted that night. It will be held in the high school auditorium on October 25 from 7:30 pm to 9:00 pm. Refreshments will be served. All are welcome.

Good Samaritan Club meeting

On Friday evening at 7:00 Jerome, Raymond and eight of their friends arrived carrying takeout containers of Indian curries. They quickly set up some tables and chairs with cutlery and started eating. It smelled so good. They offered me some but I had already had my dinner. It was wonderful hanging out with them while they chatted over their dinner. After dinner, I asked them what their plans were: they suggested some prayer time together and time to discuss issues of the day and plan their meetings. I suggested that we discuss the parable of the Good Samaritan today. We could in subsequent meetings read and discuss other Gospel teachings and how we should live out the teachings. I also asked them to formulate what they needed from the Church. I suggested that each meeting begin with a short prayer service and while I could lead the first one, I hoped that they would take the lead afterwards. Ending with tea and dessert was also a good idea.

Saturday evening after dinner I had a phone call from Colin McNeil requesting to come by at my convenience. He wanted to talk and get some advice. We agreed on Monday evening at 7:00 pm in the rectory.

CHAPTER 53

Preach: Jonah (Saturday/ Sunday, October 06/07)

Dear friends, today I wish to tell you the story of Jonah. He was a prophet that God called to go to a neighbouring city called Nineveh. This city was known for its wicked ways and to have no part with God. Jonah was to preach, "40 more days and Nineveh will be destroyed." But instead he booked passage on a ship going in the opposite direction, going west towards Spain. Soon God sends a horrible storm and everyone feels for their lives. The sailors start throwing their cargo overboard in the hope of saving themselves. Jonah is now sleeping in the bottom of the boat. In desperation, the sailors caste lots to ascertain who is causing the problem. The lot points to Jonah and he questioned. Has he offended his God? Jonah admits that he is running away from his God. The captain and the sailors now begin to pray to Jonah's God too. Jonah suggests that they throw him overboard to save themselves which they do. God however, is protecting Jonah and sends a large fish who swallows him. Jonah remains in the belly of this fish for three days until he is burped out on dry land. This time Jonah complies with God; he preaches to the Ninevites; all including the King put on sackcloth and ashes and do penance. The Kings orders that no one, no person, no animal or flock can eat or drink during the fast. All of Nineveh turns to Jonah's God. Jonah however is depressed because God is so forgiving. He was hoping for the destruction of Nineveh.

Jonah represents each one us. God calls us and we avoid him and his call; we get too busy and we have excuses. But like with Jonah, God persists and may even use extraordinary measures to achieve his objectives.

1). God is companionable and continues to engage humans in his plan for salvation; this time it is Jonah's turn;

2). In spite of God choosing the Israelite people as his special people, his ultimate plan was for all mankind, including the Assyrians, to benefit from his love, compassion and benevolence. God's love and compassion is not earned but is freely given. This was a difficult pill for the leaders of the Israelites to swallow;

3). Everyone including the captain and sailors on the ship as well as the Ninevites, their animals and flocks respond by praying to Jonah's God; and

4). God was involved in every stage of Jonah's life as a prophet even when he was running away. God is protective and solicitous even using extraordinary measures such as a whale to save and protect Jonah.

5). Like Jonah, we need to guard against becoming angry when good things happen to others that we do not think are deserved.

6). Jonah is like us. God calls, we avoid with excuses or get too busy. God persists. God works beyond the boundaries of the Catholic Church.

CHAPTER 54

Day off (Monday, October 08)

The Bishop emailed me that he wanted to have a telephone chat with me early Friday morning at 9:00 am my time. Could I make myself available? Yes, I replied.

Monday evening at 7:00 pm. A gentleman knocked on my door and introduced himself as Colin McNeil. After the usual pleasantries, I asked him what brought him here this evening. He began by saying this he lives in the community and is the high school history teacher. He is married and his wife's name is Marion. He was raised a Catholic but his first marriage ended in divorce. His first wife lives in Ottawa and has the two boys. He has remarried to Marion who was also divorced and their family consists of two girls from her previous marriage and a third child, a girl, the product of their marriage. (I did not think any humorous comments of this fellow living with four girls would be appropriate). They have lived in the community for ten years and love it here. He has missed going to Mass and wants to get back to church. How could you help me? I have tried the annulment route but I was told that we were validly married as we were both baptized Catholics. Neither of us can claim not to have given our full consent nor were not fully aware of what we were getting in.

After a moment or two of silence, Colin continued. We, that is my first wife and I were born and raised in Ontario. I studied history in university with the goal of teaching. My father was a teacher and really loved teaching. My wife became disappointed in the lifestyle a teacher's salary could only provide. She was raised with virtually anything she wanted. So, one day, Margaret was her name, she took our daughters and moved back in with her parents in Ottawa. They were happy with the move as they complained about not seeing the grandchildren often enough. I moved west in the hopes of starting over. I met Marion at a ballroom dance class in the city. We hit it off right away; perhaps we were just both lonely birds. She was a single parent with two little girls. We got married and moved here. Marion's husband had a drinking problem and abandoned the family. He supposedly lives in Vancouver. We love the small-town life; we have made friends here. The girls love it. I would like to raise our girls as Catholics.

After another silence, he asked, "How is my time?". "Fine", I replied. "It is only 7:45 and I do not go to bed until 11:00 pm. Please continue". He began by raising something that has been bothering him so some time. Suppose I have killed someone. I could go to confession and receive Holy communion, right? Yes, I assured him. But, he continued, if I get a divorce, there is no forgiveness, no second chances. I have no control over what Margaret does. I was a victim in this divorce. Divorce seems to be a bigger crime than murder. Does that seem right to you? I replied that he was right. It was not logical. I needed time, however, to consult on this matter.

Father in heaven, please inspire me to fully understand Colin's problem. Send your Holy Spirit to give me wisdom and compassion to ask the right questions, consult the right people and respond the right way with Colin and Marion.

CHAPTER 55

Scripture class "Hosea" (Tuesday, October 09)

Summary of class notes

The story of Hosea is found in the Book of Hosea. It was written during 735-732 BCE. Prophets were inspired preachers. They reminded the Israelites of their moral and ethical responsibilities, that arose from their special covenant relationship with Yahweh. They were tough dudes and boldly rebuked vice, political corruption, oppression, idolatry and moral degeneracy. Hosea was one of the minor prophets along with Amos and Micah. In fact, Hosea is a contemporary of Amos. Both prophesied in the northern kingdom of Israel. While Amos was known as a prophet of divine justice (justice in the strict sense of punishment equal to the seriousness of the crime), Hosea was known as the prophet of divine mercy and love. He used many human metaphors to explain God's love for mankind. The focus of his message is that the spiritual relationship between Yahweh and Israel is like a binding agreement or a covenant or a marriage contract. It includes a bond and requires trustworthiness like marriage. Hosea is the first prophet to use the analogy of marriage love to the covenant, a love that is willing to suffer to win back one's spouse. even an adulterous spouse. Hosea exposes Israel's relationship with pagan gods as apostasy, idolatry and infidelity. While the details are unclear, Hosea marries Gomer but who eventually becomes unfaithful. It seems that she might have been a temple prostitute. Yahweh asks Hosea to take back Gomer in spite of her infidelities. Homer's marriage with

Gomer becomes the prophet's symbol of Yahweh's relationship with Israel. Hosea understood that in the covenant, Yahweh bound himself to Israel as that of a husband to his wife in marriage regardless of the consequences. The requirements for the fulfillment of the marriage are loyalty of affection, a continuing growth in the personal knowledge of one's partner and the willingness to compensate for their infidelities, their deficiencies and their errors.

CHAPTER 56

Prepare for October 24 Deanery meeting (Wednesday, October 10)

Agenda: 12:00 to 12:45 lunch and chat
12:45 to 1:30 Church business, Bishop leads
1:30 to 3:00 pm: Christian marriage

a) Introduction of couples,
b) What do they want/need from the Church to be a happy couple and have a happy family life?
c) What is special about a Catholic marriage as opposed to a non-Catholic marriage,
d) How can a parish be more supportive of couples and families as they deal with the complexities of work, children, sports, school, illness and aging parents?
   date nights and weekends away?
e) Book club: discussion on marriage,

CHAPTER 57

Men's Group, Men's Issues
(Thursday, October 11)

There was no particular agenda established before the meeting. Fred' brought up the subject of men's health. Men do not live as long as women. He inquired if we could organize some lectures given by health care professionals on subjects like heart health. Fred said that he had heard that when men get old, they cannot pee. What about prostate health? Other suggestions like digestive health, vitamins and exercise. Fred agreed to phone the hospital for some direction. Bill inquired about a cooking course for men only. I agreed to tackle that subject and Bill agreed to phone the hospital to see if we could rent their kitchen when they were finished for the day.

Father in heaven, the men's club are becoming my friends who talk about some very personal matters. Thank you for them.

CHAPTER 58

Office work/study(Friday, October 12)

At 9:00 am sharp on Friday morning, Bishop Ben phoned to say that he had met the Cardinal in Toronto at a dinner during the week. The Cardinal had mentioned that his friend, Ed Malone wanted to do a feature article about the two of us for the Toronto Tribune. He was very re-assuring about Ed's reliability and he has encouraged us to cooperate. He thought that Ed would give us considerable editorial control over the content just as he did with me when he did an article for the Tribune when I arrived in Toronto. Please have Ed phone Margaret to set up two appointments, one for me alone and one for both of us. He hung up thanking me and stating that could not talk further as he was late for another meeting.

CHAPTER 59

Preach "Change in the Church" (Saturday/Sunday, October 13/14)

Dear friends, today, I would like to chat with you about change in the church. Some of you fear change and prefer a very predictable lifestyle. Unfortunately, change is everywhere is our lives. As adults, we grow old and cannot do all the things we used to do. Our children grow up and leave to our regret. Change is a part of life. Learning to accept the things we cannot change makes for a happier life.

Change in the Catholic Church is painful for some. I do not understand that pain and discomfort. Perhaps it is because change can result in pain and disharmony. Looking back through history, the church supported slavery and banned usury or the loaning money at interest. More recently, the Second Vatican Council changed the language of the liturgy from Latin to English, encouraged the singing of hymns long associated with Protestant churches and brought the altar closer to the people as a gesture of inclusiveness. After a period of adjustment, these changes seem like second nature.

The sexual abuse crises in the church has raised the

question again of married men priests and female married or single women priests. I meet with the Anglican and Baptist ministers, both females, in town. They are very effective leaders of their congregations and well liked. A male celibate clergy is a church regulation and can be changed. In the early church, it was known that St. Peter, the leader of the apostles and the first pope, was married. Given the shortage of celibate male priests particularly in remote areas like the Amazon, there is a call for the ordination of what are called men of proven virtue. Celibacy will continue to be practiced in men's and women's monasteries.

I regretfully and sadly admit, that women are not being considered for ordination in the Catholic church. There are some who say the male leadership of the Church have done so much damage over the years, that it is time for the leadership to be turned over to women. It is not widely known that many parishes in the United States are administered by women and religious sisters.

On a personal note, I was called to the priesthood later in life by our God of surprises, so I believe that God is in charge of the church. Whatever he is planning for his Church, it will be enough for us to develop a loving and beneficial relationship with God and our fellow men and women.

CHAPTER 60

Day off (Monday, October 15)

I phoned Jerome today to inquire if the Good Samaritan Club would put on a basic cooking course for the men in the parish. I explained that this was part of the willingness of these men to be more responsible at home. He agreed to consult with others members of the club and get back to me. He asked if lesbians could join the club as they have been approached by a small group of them. Good idea but I need to consult too.

CHAPTER 61

Scripture Class "Ruth" (Tuesday, October 16)

Summary of class notes

The story of Ruth is found in the Book of Ruth. The story takes place in the period of the Judges around 1100 BCE and appears to have been written between 950 and 700 BCE. It is a beautiful story of "chesed", translated as loyalty and faithfulness to a commitment. During a famine, Elimelech and Naomi and their two sons move to nearby Moab to live. While there, the two boys take Moab wives, Orpah and Ruth. Meanwhile, all three men die leaving the three women to fend for themselves. Naomi suggests that both widows return to their respective families. Orpah agrees but Ruth decides to remain with Naomi. Ruth's statement of loyalty is famous, "Do not press me to leave you or to turn back from following you; Where you go, I will go; where you lodge, I will lodge; your people will be my people, and your God my God. Where you die, I will die- there will I be buried. May the Lord do thus and so to me and more as well, if even death parts me from you!" Then Naomi and Ruth return to Bethlehem to rebuild their lives. Ruth asks Naomi's permission go to pick up left over grain on the field of Boaz, a wealthy relative of her husband Elimelech.

Ruth meets Boaz and the relationship blossoms. Boaz realizing Ruth's situation, calls a meeting of the town's elders where he proposes to purchase the land of the deceased relative and marry Ruth if there are no extended family members willing to do so. No one comes forward and Boaz and Ruth are married and have a son Obed. Obed is part of the lineage of Christ. There are three main characters in this story that demonstrate "chesed" translated as loyalty or fidelity to a commitment:

a) Naomi shows "chesed" to her widowed daughter-in-law Ruth by looking out for her, while she has no obligation to do so;

b) Ruth shows "chesed" by caring and supporting Naomi beyond expectations and by seeking a marriage with Boaz, the family protector.

c) Boaz exhibits "chesed" by showing hospitality and security to Ruth beyond the legal requirements, when he coaches his workers to leave some grain in the field for the poor, including Ruth, as is required by the law. He further exhibits this loyalty when he accepts the double responsibility of a land purchase and a marriage thereby preserving the lineage and inheritance of a family that were almost lost.

Takeaways: Loyalty to God and family, generosity to the less fortunate, playing by societies rules and hard work are acknowledged.

CHAPTER 62

Meeting with
my Protestant Colleagues
(Wednesday, October 17)

Our second meeting at St. Francis included an update by Ed on the Public Service Appreciation Night. a typical Buddhist meditation on mindfulness, details of the Civic Appreciation Night. Ed was voted in as chair of the group. He advised that the Mayor wants to be the master of ceremonies. He will read out the profiles of each of the recipients, who will then come forward individually to receive a trophy and a photo with the Mayor. After all the recipients have been acknowledged and feted, we will socialize and eat. The food is being prepared by women from the three parishes.

Don Keating then gave a short but very interesting talk on compassion and wisdom from a Buddhist perspective. In Buddhism, the mind is the key to enlightenment or everlasting happiness. An important part of Buddhism especially Mahayana Buddhism, is the development of the mind. In practice, the core teaching is helping or serving others without selfish motivation. We are to open our minds and bodies to others.

To help others, we must develop an enlightened mind. An enlightened mind understands that all beings, humans, animals and even insects can become enlightened. An enlightened mind is calm and clear. It is free from disturbances from external events, emotional struggles and rigid ways of looking at the world around us. The more peaceful the mind becomes, the more it gains in wisdom and clarity.

The enlightened mind can see everything as unified or as one. There is no dualism or I- you or we-them. We are interconnected. Harming someone or something, is harming ourselves.

The opposite of a calm and clear mind is one resulting from our current lifestyle of acquisitions. Success is having a prosperous life; big house, car and weekend home. It thrives on financial ambition and opportunities. It can result in an elevated sense of self and power over others. The success can also result in stress and anxiety as well as negative emotions. A calm and clear mind is achieved through meditation. During meditation, we free ourselves from intellectual and emotional obscureness.

Father in heaven, thank you for this small group of volunteers who are dedicated to making the world a better place. Help us to open our hearts to a different spiritual path and our minds to appreciate these differences.

CHAPTER 63

Pastoral Council meeting (Thursday, October 18)

Tonight, the re-constituted Parish Council met for the first time. There were ten attendees, five women, five men, with representatives from both the CWL and the men's group and me. Fred brought the meeting to order. I updated everyone on the status of parish activities: the Good Samaritan Club, the Civic Appreciation Night, the Anglicans are still considering sharing our church space but nothing was final (I informed the Pastoral Council that I had passed on their suggested requirements to

Rev. Claire and Bishop Ben), my Inter-denominational group's activities, the upcoming Deanery meeting topic of Christian Marriage and the three couples that have consented to join us in this workshop format and Ed Malone's upcoming article in the Toronto Tribune on Bishop Ben and myself.

I then presented Colin McNeil's situation to them without identifying him or his family. I presented his background and his challenge to the teaching on divorce, especially the Church's willingness to forgive a murderer but not a divorced person. Fred asked me if I was talking about Colin McNeil and that it is hard to keep secrets in a small town. The parish knew his situation and were very concerned and sympathetic. Fred asked me to explain the church's position on divorce. The prohibition of divorce goes way back to the time of Adam and Eve, Moses and Mosaic law. This law stipulated that a man could only divorce his wife if she was unfaithful. Christ extended the divorce prohibition to all marriages except to those that were within prohibited blood lines. He further explained that Moses only allowed divorce because of the hardness of the Israelite's hearts. I explained the annulment process, the Pauline privilege, the Eastern Orthodox Church's rule of tolerating one divorce in one's lifetime, the various Protestant Church's opposition to divorce and remarriage ranges from never to adultery only to adultery and abandonment and finally Hosea's teaching on marital relationships which could be interpreted as never. Fred wanted to know what the Bishop and my priests' colleagues would say to Colin. I said that they would probably say that these are the rules that Catholics must live by. Colin and Marion can go to the sacraments provided they agree to live like brother and sister. The quiet laughter in the room erupted. Bill asked why there was a discrepancy among the Christian churches if all use the same Bible for their direction? I answered that I did not know. Ned asked me if I ever slept brother and sister with a sexy woman that you loved? More laughter. Fred added that in his opinion, a woman's sex drive increased as they got older. More laughter now at my expense. It seems to me, Fred continued, that the Church was depriving this couple of the loving and emotional support that marriage can provide to couples. Liz's comment was that the divorce prohibition would make sense in the time of Moses, but not given the different conditions of our society. Thelma commented that perhaps one should only enter a civil marriage or a common law marriage rather than getting tangled up in the legal technicalities of a Christian marriage. I then thanked Liz and Thelma for their astute comments. I asked what the others felt about this teaching on the prohibition of divorce. They all murmured that the teaching seemed to be terribly onerous and very unforgiving. Mabel said that Colin's comparison about divorce and murder was very thought-provoking. Ned spoke up saying that Colin was an excellent history teacher, had taught his girls, was a community volunteer and even sat on Town Council for one year until Marion became pregnant. After a short debate, they concluded that I should present Colin's case to the Bishop and that the Pastoral Council thinks that Colin, Marion and the girls should be welcomed into the parish community and allowed to receive all the sacraments they desire. Why? If the government is not welcome in our bedrooms, why is the Church. Christ welcomed outsiders into his small community and instructed us not to judge.

Father in heaven, this pastoral council is very definitive in support for Colin, Marian and their girls. I trust their judgment here. If it is true that they are a loving couple and family, then God must be present in their lives. Thank you.

CHAPTER 64

Good Samaritan Club meeting
(Friday, October 19)

The second meeting of the Good Samaritan Club was as interesting as the first. After putting their food in my oven to keep warm, we began with a prayer, the Our Father. To prepare ourselves to be in the presence of our Father in heaven, we made a small examination of conscience and asked for his forgiveness. Jerome read the story of the Good Samaritan and a very animated discussion followed. They identified with both characters, the victim beaten and robbed and the good Samaritan himself. They all had stories of these type of experiences. Very cathartic. When asked what they want from the Church, they wanted to be treated like everyone else, nothing special. They wanted to be supported in getting married and the adopting and raising of children. I also told them that given the high divorce rate, I am very interested in promoting strong marital and family relationships. They quickly responded that they would like to participate in such workshops or activities if allowed. I also asked what they could do for the Church and society. Big silence. I asked them based on the smells of their dinner today and their curries last time, if they like to cook. They were unanimous; they love to cook. I asked them if they would teach me and some of the men in parish; they were unanimous in consent. Wow. The meeting ended with a nice Italian dinner comprised of risotto, chicken cacciatore, a medley of fresh vegetables and bottles of a German white Riesling. Those guys really know how to party.

Father in heaven, thank you for this opportunity to be of service here. These men are so gentle, kind and sensitive. Please keep them safe.

CHAPTER 65

Preach on the "Story of Ruth" (Saturday/Sunday, October 20/21)

Dear friends, I would like to share with you what I learned about a woman named Ruth. Her beautiful story, even though is short, is a separate book in the Old Testament. Her story highlights loyalty and faithfulness to a commitment. During a famine, a married couple, Elimelech and Naomi and their two sons migrate to a neighbouring country called Moab. While there, the two sons take non-Jewish wives, Orpah and Ruth. Soon, all three men, Elimelech and his two sons die, leaving the three women to fend for themselves. Women in this situation at that time as there was no social welfare, usually became beggars. Naomi realizing that she cannot survive in a foreign land, decides to return to Bethlehem. She suggests that her two daughters-in-law, being Moabites, should return to their families for their economic survival. Orpah complied, but Ruth chose to remain with Naomi. Her request to remain is a beautiful poetic request. Ruth said, "Do not press me to leave or to turn back from following you. Where you will go, I will go; where you lodge, I will lodge; your people will be my people, and your God my God. Where you die, I will die, there I will be buried. May the Lord do thus and so to me, and more as well."

Back in Bethlehem, Naomi decides to sell the land that she and her former husband owned. She also advises Ruth to collect the leftover grain in the fields by the harvesters of a distant relative, Boaz. Farmers were encouraged by Jewish law, to leave grain in the fields for the poor. Ruth was able in this way, to care for her mother-in-law.

Boaz, realizing that Naomi's land was for sale, approached

the town's elders to discuss the potential purchase. He also informed the elders that according to the Levirate law, the land purchase also included caring for Ruth. This law meant that when a married man died, a brother or male relative of the deceased should marry the widow and have children in the deceased's name to protect the integrity of the family. As no male relatives came forward, this example is not a perfect example of this law. As no one wanted the land or to take for Ruth, Boaz purchased the land and married Ruth. They had a son called Obed, who was the grandfather of King David.

This story celebrates Naomi's loyalty to Ruth and not abandoning her. Ruth's loyalty and care for Naomi, her mother-in-law. Boaz's loyalty in purchasing the land and marrying Ruth who in turn would continue to care for Naomi.

Takeaways:

1. Contrary to other stories we have talked about, God is not an active person in the story except in Ruth's poetic commitment to Naomi and her Jewish religion and culture.
2. While God is not an active person in the story, God is implicitly present. The loyalty expressed by these three people is rooted in goodness and love, the source of which is God. There is no dualism in the story; all these three characters are inter-connected as one.
3. Loyalty pays off. I am reminded when I purchase gas for my car at a Husky station to use my loyalty for points that I do not collect.

CHAPTER 66

Day off (Monday, October 22)

Sunday night dinner with the family, sleeping in my old bed and some uninterrupted scripture study time occupied most of my day off with mother. I had dinner with Father Mike and arrived back at 9:00 pm to catch up on some NFL sporting news. Father, thank you for giving me this good life.

CHAPTER 67

Scripture class "Tobit" (Tuesday, October 23)

Summary of class notes:

The story of Tobit is found in the Book of Tobit in the Old Testament. It is a fictional account of life in biblical times. It is estimated to have been written between 250 and 200 BCE. It illustrates God's providential activity within the setting of marriage and family life but particularly so of Jewish life in captivity. The story stresses the importance of a Jewish man finding a spouse from within Judaism. There are two stories; one of Tobit in Nineveh and a second of Sarah who lives in Ecbatana. Tobit is described as a meticulous follower of the Mosaic law while living in Israel and in Nineveh in Assyria. While still living in Israel, he gave the first portion of his harvest and herds to the Temple in Jerusalem, he gave 10% of his wealth to the Levites and also gave money for the poor and the widows. While in captivity, he continues to practice charity and buries the dead in spite enduring criticism and mockery from his countrymen and from the Assyrian rulers.

As the story begins, Tobit, his wife Anna and his son Tobias are in captivity in Nineveh. He first establishes his Jewish heritage back to one of the twelve tribes, Naphtali. One evening after burying someone, he sleeps in his courtyard and during the night the droppings of sparrows fall on his eyes, causing him to go blind. Like a lot of men, he does not handle losing control well. After a disagreement with Anna, he prays for death. Putting his estate in order, he remembers the money left in trust with Gabael at Ragas in Media. He asks his son Tobias to find a companion who can escort him to Ragas. He finds the angel Raphael who disguised as a man named Azarias, who agrees to be his companion.

The story of Sarah is full of tragedy. She has had seven marriages, but on all of these wedding nights, the husbands had died before the marriages could be consummated, leaving her childless and a disgrace in the community. She decides to hang herself but changes her mind not wanting to shame her father. She now prays for an early death.

Tobias on his journey catches a large fish and with Azarias' advice keeps the gall, the heart and the liver. Why keep them? The smoke from burning the heart and the liver will scare off the demon from a man or woman. The gall can be used as an anointment to remove the film from someone's eyes. They arrive at Raguel's house and Sarah's parents think Tobias and Sarah would make a wonderful couple. Azarias leaves to acquire the trust money. Upon his return, Azarias encourages the marriage plans in spite of Tobias' fear of becoming number eight. Azarias reminds Tobias of the heart and liver and the benefits of the smoke. Tobias follows Azarias' instructions and the marriage is consummated. The three, Tobias, Sarah and

Azarias return to Nineveh where Tobias uses the gall ointment to cure his father's blindness.

Takeaways:

1. God blesses someone who is dutiful, charitable and faithful to the law.
2. There is unjust suffering, the unseen demonic realm causes the innocent of suffer.
3. God sends suffering to those who are law-abiding and virtuous but only as a temporary means of self-improvement.
4. Things end well for the just and virtuous suffering person.
5. A sovereign and just God is active, orchestrating events for the good of those who are virtuous and law-abiding.
6. God blesses a faith that is expressed in acts of love and kindness.
7. Divine providence will overcome the obstacles that faithful couples face in marriage and family life.

CHAPTER 68

Deanery meeting on Christian Marital love (Wednesday, October 24)

The Deanery meeting lunch began with Indian curries prepared by Fr. Raj Patel. The lunch included Dal, Persian rice, Naan bread, chicken curry and a mixed vegetable curry. It was delightful. The Bishop updated us on his recent meetings with the Bishops of Canada. He indicated that he is asking the priests in his diocese to be more accommodating in their pastoral activities. His one example was the story of the

Good Samaritan Club in my parish. He also mentioned that the Toronto Tribune, a national paper, was doing a feature story on him and the diocese. When I took over the meeting, I asked my colleagues how they get their parishioners into a deeper relationship with God. The Bishop jumped in to rescue me as my three married couples were entering the meeting room. After introductions and tea all around, I asked my three couples what they needed from the Church to have a happy relationship as a couple and as a family. Fred jumped in by saying that this subject has been an item of discussion in both the CWL and the Men's group in the parish. Making it an item that is talked about in the parish is an important first step. A strong parish community where families care for one another's children would be the first step in helping couples to get away for an occasional weekend of time alone. Mabel suggested that a weekend retreat for couples where the couples themselves give talks on various subjects. We know better than priests do what works and does not work in a marriage. We would invite a psychologist to contribute on contentious matters. The Bishop stated that this idea was wonderful and he would put diocesan energy behind it. He asked the three couples if they would help him. They happily agreed. Their question to us was, what makes a Catholic marriage as opposed to a non-Catholic marriage? Fr. George said that he thought that forgiveness, a very special Christian principle played an important part. Fr. Raj added that he thought that the Christian attitude to suffering was also important. He indicated that Christians see suffering as a learning opportunity to broaden our parameters of what loving means. Suffering and forgiveness can get us over the hump of a crises. I told them the back story to Hosea who was asked by God to reconcile with his wife who had been unfaithful. Just as God loves us and forgives our many failures, so, we need to love and forgive those in our daily lives who disappoint and offend us. The meeting was a big success. Everyone including the Bishop thought that this group should meet again to flesh out further the ideas discussed today.

The Bishop emailed me saying that he apologized for cutting off my inquiry of getting our parishioners motivated into deeper spiritual lives. He suggested that we might try to use the internet and emails to include all members of the Deanery.

Father in heaven, thank you for another wonderful day in your service. Please care for Bishop Ben, the priests and the members of the parish who participated today.

CHAPTER 69

Pastoral challenges and successes (Thursday, October 25)

Ed Malone arrived at my door during my breakfast with his tape recorder wanting some interview time. He has finished with his interviews with the Bishop but needed more time with me. He squeezed an hour and a half of my time and left, saying that he would see me tonight at the Public Service Appreciation night. He was definitely on a mission.

I wrote a long email to the Bishop and copied Fr. Mike about Colin's marital situation.

The Public Service Appreciation Night was a huge success with a big crowd. The Mayor spoke eloquently about the honorees before having their photos taken. Ed was front and center during all this, looking for material for future articles for his newspaper. The Mayor thanked the organizers, asked us to stand and take a bow with more photos.

Father in heaven, thank you for helping to organize such a wonderful community event. It gave everyone a lift.

CHAPTER 70

Bishop Ben is special
(Friday, October 26)

The Bishop emailed me back this morning. It was surprisingly a short response. He stated that he talked with Father Mike yesterday after he had read my email. They both expressed sympathy for Colin, Marian and their family circumstances. They both felt that the theology on marriage and divorce needed a major review and even overhaul. In the meantime, they should be advised with your help to become as fully informed as possible and then to review the options and decide with a clear conscience. If they present themselves for communion at a parish in the city, no one will know their circumstances. They will be fine. If they present themselves for communion in your church, you should treat them as you would any other parishioner. Remember, "who are we to judge?" The Bishop continued that he remembered as a priest in Ecuador, I suspected there were many people who came to church at Easter and Christmas who were in what we used to call irregular marriages. Who would know? We never suspected. No one complained.

I immediately phoned Colin and Marion's home. Marion answered. I asked if she and Colin would be at home this evening and could I come by for a short visit with good news. She responded yes, please come by at 9:00 pm after their children were in bed.

At 9:00 pm, I was welcomed by them into their home. I relayed the Bishop's message. They were delighted but wondered how the people in St. Francis would react even with an explanation. I outlined the content of the recent Pastoral

Council meeting in which they felt the church's official teaching on divorce and remarriage was too severe. They think that we should welcome you with open arms. I agreed too. I left them with the option of letting them adjust to the good news and then to phone me any time to chat about how all this should unfold. They agreed. They also gave me their permission to share their full story with the Pastoral Council.

Father in heaven, another glorious day of working in your church. Who could have guessed how great this family is tonight? Thank you for Bishop Ben and Fr. Mike. Continue to care for Colin and Marion and their children.

CHAPTER 71

Preach "The story of Tobit" (Saturday/Sunday, October 27/28)

Dear friends, I would like to chat with you about the Book of Tobit in the Old Testament. It has interesting lessons for us. The story takes place between 700 and 500 BCE. The main characters of the story are Jewish but are living in captivity as exiles in a foreign country.

One main character is Tobit who started life as a child orphan and then as a young man, was carried off to Nineveh in Assyria. Assyria is what today is known as northern Iraq and southeastern Turkey. The Assyrians only tolerate the Jewish refugees. Tobit is married to Anna and they have a son Tobias. Tobit is very religious, makes regular pilgrimages to Jerusalem to worship, financially supports the temple and gives money to the poor. In Nineveh, he cares for the poor and risks his life to bury fellow Jews who are victims of persecution. As a result, he receives death threats, the threat of confiscation of his property, the ridicule of his neighbors and even the scorn of his wife. One evening after a burial, he slept outside his house in accordance with the purification rules of the Mosaic Law and was blinded by bird droppings. He now prays for death and organizes his estate. He gives directions to his son Tobias to journey to Rhages in Media where his inheritance money is stored. Media is what is known today as Kurdistan.

Another main character is young woman, named Sarah. She is living in exile in Ecbatana, the capital of Media. She is an only child and has suffered terribly. On seven occasions, her future spouses have died on their wedding night before their marriage could be consummated. A demon was causing these deaths. She too was praying for death to end her suffering.

God heard both the prayers of Tobit and Sarah and sends his angel Raphael, disguised as a relative Azarias to help them. Azarias leads Tobias and his dog to Ecbatana. On route they catch a large fish and Azarias shows Tobias how to cut out it's gall, heart and liver. The gall will heal blindness and the heart and liver will heal someone afflicted by an evil spirit or demon. Azarias explains that Sarah is a kinswoman of his and he is entitled to marry her. He is apprehensive having heard of the previous seven husbands. On their wedding night, Tobias and Sarah burn the heart and liver which chases away the demon and the marriage is consummated. He soon returns home with a wife and his inheritance and cures his father's blindness with the gall of the fish. There is a happy ending to this story.

Tobit unsure if he will ever see Tobias again, gives him parental instructions on how to live, care for his mother and devotedly to practice their Jewish faith. They are beautiful and are found in chapter 4, verses 1-19.

What are the takeaways:

1. God blesses and protects those who practice acts of love with family, friends and community.
2. God helps couples overcome obstacles in marriage and family life.
3. God is a companion with those who suffer and who call out to him for help.

CHAPTER 72

Day off (Monday, October 29)

Mother cooked my favorite dinner last evening; roast beef, roasted vegetables of potatoes, turnip and corn and pumpkin pie. My sister razed me all evening about my weight gain, my tight looking clothes and my tired looking eyes. She wondered if I was watching too much late-night TV and getting sleep-deprived. To put her back on her heels, I alerted them about the feature article of Bishop Ben and me in the Toronto Tribune. Sis then inquired if I was being groomed to become a bishop. Bishop Cam has a nice ring to it. Finally, mother came to my rescue and politely asked her to give this hard-working family member a break. Thank goodness for families.

Monday was a rest day in my parent's home, breakfast and a walk with mother, study time, dinner with Fr. Mike and home for an NFL weekend summary. A good day.

CHAPTER 73

Scripture class "Esther" (Tuesday, October 30)

Summary of class notes

The story of Esther is found in the Book of Esther in the Old Testament. It takes place between 533 and 333 BCE. The key characters are Esther, an orphan Jewish woman and her uncle Mordecai who live in exile in Babylon. The Babylonian Empire now extends from Iraq to India. Jerusalem was destroyed and the remaining Jewish people are in exile in Persia in what is today known as Iraq.

1. The story begins with a six-month drinking feast given by King Ahasuerus for all his officials and his large army. There is also a seven-day drinking feast for his subjects. During the party, Ahasuerus becomes inebriated and orders his wife to display her beauty and appear naked. As she has skin condition, she refuses and is removed as Queen.
2. After a long search, Ahasuerus chooses Esther as his Queen. She does not reveal her Jewishness
3. Haman is appointed by the King as his viceroy. Mordecai offends Haman by refusing to acknowledge his new elevated status and bow to him in the streets. Upon discovering that Mordecai is Jewish, he arranges with the King's agreement to have all Jewish people, men, women and children killed.
4. Mordecai learns of this plot and requests that Esther appeal to the King. She refuses and alerts Mordecai that if she approaches the King without being called, she will be put to death.

5. Esther relents and begins a three-day period of fasting and prayer. She also asks Mordecai to request all the Jewish people to do the same.
6. Mordecai discovers a plot by two of the palace guards to kill the King. With his help, they are apprehended and hanged. Mordecai's service to the King is officially recorded.
7. Haman is offended again by Mordecai's refusal to bow to him in the streets and on his wife's advice orders gallows to be built immediately to hang Mordecai.
8. Esther organizes two feasts for the King and Haman. Between these two feasts, the King has a sleepless night and has the daily court records read to him to put him to sleep. He discovers Mordecai's life-saving effort and inquires what has been done for Mordecai to reward him for his good deed. He was told nothing.
9. When Haman arrives for the second celebration, the King asks him what he would do to honor someone. Haman replies that such a person should be dressed in royal robes and led around on the King's royal horse. The King agrees and to Haman's horror, he orders Haman to render such honors to Mordecai.
10. During the second banquet feting the King and Haman, Esther reveals that she is Jewish and Haman's plans to exterminate her people including her. The Kings orders that Haman be hung immediately.
11. Mordecai and Esther write another decree overruling the earlier one. Mordecai becomes the King's viceroy and institutes an annual feast called Purim, celebrating the saving of the Jewish people from death.
12. Purim is celebrated by:

- Exchanging gifts of food and drink;
- Donating to the poor and needy;
- Having a celebratory meal, and;
- A public recitation of Esther's story with prayers and grace after meals.

CHAPTER 74

Toronto Tribune Feature Story by Ed Malone (Wednesday, October 31)

I n a small rural prairie community in Western Canada, known as the hinterland by most easterners, there is a two-man team of religious leaders that is quietly transforming the spiritual and community landscape. (Note: The two gentlemen-clerics have unfortunately requested anonymity and the editors of the Tribune have reluctantly complied). This team is made up of a Roman Catholic Bishop and a newly-minted priest in his diocese. They are not miracle workers but rather typical modest Westerners when you first meet them. They are very quiet listeners that believe in organizing strong parish organizations that contribute to the wider community.

The Bishop is known for being quite ordinary and down to earth. He lives in a small two-bedroom apartment, rents office space nearby, celebrates a 7:00 am mass most mornings at the Cathedral, lunches at the Cathedral with whomever turns up for lunch, cooks his own evening meals when possible (preferably Italian) and has a black Labrador dog, named Max as his companion. While he normally wears a simple black suit with a roman collar, he is a CFL fan and is often seen wearing a CFL team jersey on a game day. He wears a small wooden cross (not silver or fancy), given to him by a good friend, a Franciscan monk from Ecuador. According to some of priests in his diocese, he is very unpretentious and a good listener. He was born in Northern Alberta to a Metis father and a French-Canadian mother. Father worked in the oil patch and mother was a teacher. After high school, the Bishop worked for an oil services company in Northern Alberta before being transferred to Texas. At a weekend mass, he heard a priest from Ecuador, South America, talk about the shortage of priests. He joined the Society of St Paul, a North American order of priests working in South America. Assigned to a large inner-city parish in Quito, he spent seven years organizing small urban schools in low income communities. Pope Francis named him a Bishop for this diocese because of ability with languages; he speaks Dene, French, English and Spanish.

The Priest is an interesting person. He studied social work at university, built affordable housing and emergency woman's shelters, was married but lost his wife at a very young age to ALS and then decided to become a Catholic priest. After being assigned to a rural parish, he has encouraged his parishioners to focus on making the community a better place to live. He has activated a number of parish organizations. He started an Inter-denominational group of religious leaders in the community that is organizing an Appreciation Night for staff of the local hospital, the schools, the RCMP and Town Office. His parish has taken on the responsibility of parks maintenance and clean-up of public areas in the community. When I interviewed some of his parishioners for this article, they praised him for his outreach, his inclusiveness, his promotion of marriage and family life and his short, punchy sermons.

I also had an opportunity to interview them together. The Bishop kicked off the conversation by saying that he was delighted to have this priest in his diocese. His married life and previous employment experience bring a fresh perspective to the pastoral work in our diocese. He is very spiritual, a team player, consultative, receptive to ideas, generous with his time and talents, confident in his abilities but also quite aware of his limitations. He is a well-rounded person. He has a motto that I admire: "Faith in actions, not words".

Father, the Bishop gave you a large vote of confidence. He gave me a second chance, which I will always be grateful for. He is a great listener. He is understated in the way he lives, quite unlike the princely lifestyle many leaders of the church feel the need to live. He manages change well, always balancing the new needs of the church with the fears of those who are opposed to change and afraid of being left behind. One thing I particularly like is when I need to bend one of the rules for a good pastoral reason, he has assured me that even though he is not able to give me permission to do so, he will always give me forgiveness. This assurance is totally new to me but so welcome. If I were to sum up, he acts like my image of how God the Father would act if he were in the Bishop's shoes, with compassion and honesty. As psalm 103 assures us "The Lord is merciful and gracious, slow to anger and abounding in steadfast love". This psalm reflects how the Bishop acts. I pray every day for him. He has a very tough job leading and managing a motley group of priests, nuns and laity.

To my question of the possibility of married priests or women priests, the Bishop stated that the Catholic Church is still committed to a celibate male priesthood, but who knows the future. If this were to occur, he would be comfortable with such a change. He concluded our conversation with a cautionary note: as my grandfather used to say, "new solutions, bring new problems."

ACKNOWLEDGEMENTS

The author wishes to thank the many friends and family who reviewed the manuscript and offered so many helpful suggestions.

The author wishes to acknowledge the following reference materials utilized to develop this story:

1. Duggan, Michael. The Consuming Fire: A Christian Guide to the Old Testament. Our Sunday Visiter, 2010.
2. Louf, André, OCSO, In the School of Contemplation, translated by Paul Rowe, OCSO, Liturgical Press. 2015.
3. The Harper Collins Study Bible including Apocryphal Deuterocanonical Books, New Revised Standard Version, Student Edition, General Editor Harold W. Attridge. New York: Harper Collins, 2006.
4. Reid, Barbara E., The Gospel According to Matthew. Liturgical Press, 2005.

The author takes full responsibility for any errors or omissions in the text. The author also wants to unequivocally state to the reader that this work is only fiction, developed in my very active imagination and that any resemblance to any person living or dead is purely an accident or a coincidence.

Manufactured by Amazon.ca
Bolton, ON

20752924R00085